Joseph Chamberlain
1836–1914

Rt. Hon. Joseph Chamberlain (photograph by Draycott, Birmingham). From Louis Creswicke, *The Life of The Right Honourable Joseph Chamberlain*, Volume 1, London, 1904.

Joseph Chamberlain 1836–1914

A Bibliography

Compiled by SCOTT NEWTON
and DILWYN PORTER

Bibliographies and Indexes in World History,
Number 32

Greenwood Press
Westport, Connecticut • London

Library of Congress Cataloging-in-Publication Data

Newton, Scott.
Joseph Chamberlain, 1836–1914 : a bibliography / compiled by Scott Newton and Dilwyn Porter.
p. cm.—(Bibliographies and indexes in world history, ISSN 0742–6852 ; no. 32)
ISBN 0–313–28290–0 (alk. paper)
1. Chamberlain, Joseph, 1836–1914—Bibliography. 2. Great Britain—Politics and government—1837–1901—Bibliography. 3. Great Britain—Politics and government—1901–1910—Bibliography.
I. Porter, Dilwyn. II. Title. III. Series.
Z8158.827N48 1994
[DA565.C4]
016.941081'092—dc20 93–50544

British Library Cataloguing in Publication Data is available.

Library of Congress Catalog Card Number: 93–50544
ISBN: 0–313–28290–0
ISSN: 0742–6852

First published in 1994

Greenwood Press, 88 Post Road West, Westport, CT 06881
An imprint of Greenwood Publishing Group, Inc.

Printed in the United States of America

The paper used in this book complies with the Permanent Paper Standard issued by the National Information Standards Organization (Z39.48–1984).

10 9 8 7 6 5 4 3 2

Contents

Preface

It was, according to Churchill, the mark of a great man "so to have handled matters during his life that the course of after events is continuously affected by what he did". Measured by this standard Joseph Chamberlain was a great man.

Having first made his mark in business Chamberlain devoted himself to public life, establishing his political base in Birmingham, a city whose industrious classes came to adopt him as "Our Joe".

It was soon clear that Chamberlain's radical instinct was not to be constrained within the framework of Gladstonian Liberalism. His spectacular career as Lord Mayor of Birmingham opened a new phase in municipal politics as the environment of the city was transformed and the facilities of progressive local government were significantly advanced by Birmingham's example and Chamberlain, even before he reached Westminster, was talked of as a future Liberal Party leader and prime minister.

After 1880 Chamberlain's passion for constructive politics was frustrated in a cabinet where the Whiggish tendency loomed large. His interest in old age pensions, however, dates from this period and he was able to issue the "Chamberlain Circular" during a brief spell at the Local Government Board in 1886, authorising a new form of relief for unemployed workers who would otherwise have been exposed to the degradation of the poor law.

By this time his relationship with his party was under stress as his loyalties were tested to the limit by Gladstone's conversion to Irish home rule, a policy which, in Chamberlain's view, threatened to undermine the sovereignty of the imperial parliament, striking a blow at the heart of empire. Chamberlain abandoned Gladstone to his obsession and led his new party, the Liberal Unionists, into a parliamentary alliance with those Conservatives who had once despised the radical demagogue from "Brummagem". These manoeuvres determined the shape of party politics in Britain for the next thirty years.

Chamberlain's final political incarnation was as a social-imperialist. Offered a seat in Salisbury's 1895 cabinet, he chose the colonial office where he pursued Britain's global interests, vigorously and controversially, notably in South Africa, until 1903. The war which ensued was very much "Chamberlain's war" fought, his critics claimed, on behalf of British capital overseas.

His determination to consolidate the British empire while, at the same time, protecting home industry and providing revenue for pensions, led him to advocate tariff reform after 1903. This was the cause for which, in Austen Chamberlain's words, "father sacrificed more than life itself". It was also the cause for which he sacrificed the unity of the Conservatives and Liberal Unionists who paid a heavy price for his last crusade. As one of his Conservative opponents, Strachey of *The Spectator*, observed, Chamberlain was "a great and patriotic Englishman, though often a very rash one".

Each phase of Chamberlain's long and many-faceted career is surveyed in this bibliography which seeks to provide a comprehensive guide for researchers and research supervisors. It is our wish that this work will prove of value to all those embarking on serious study of the man himself or the political causes to which he was devoted or, indeed, to any student immersed in the historiographic debates which he has generated. A mere handlist, no matter how extensive, is of limited use to a new researcher so we have tried to be of greater assistance by providing brief comments on each entry. Having ourselves travelled in vain on a number of occasions we have included contact addresses wherever possible to facilitate the prudent enquiry prior to a visit.

If we have perpetrated any injustices in the few words of description which we have allowed ourselves then apologies are in order. Our words are intended to encourage readers to take up the task of research for themselves if only to confound our opinions. And, of course, a little spice does cheer up what could be a rather dull pudding.

Acknowledgments

It would not have been possible to complete this project without the co-operation of libraries and archive institutions throughout the United Kingdom, Ireland and the United States. We would like to single out, however, the staff of the Local History Department at Birmingham Central Library who were unfailing in their kindness and their willingness to walk many miles, to and from the stacks, on our behalf; and Dr Ben Benedicz, Head of Special Collections, University Library, Birmingham, whose knowledge about both the Chamberlain archives and the Chamberlain family is compendious, and who was courteous and helpful to us both.

Both authors are grateful for the financial assistance provided by Worcester College through the School of Arts and Science Individual Research Fund (for Dr Porter) and by University of Wales College, Cardiff, through the School of History and Archaeology Research Fund (for Dr Newton).

The bibliography would not have been completed so (comparatively) smoothly without the enormous professionalism, patience and good humour of Beryl Richards.

The greatest debt of any author must be to the family. We both owe so much to Sandra, Daniel, Philip and Rachel Porter and to Maria Newton, who all lived patiently not just with Joseph Chamberlain but also innumerable printouts and index cards.

Chapter One

Biographical Essay

Though destined to make his mark as a man of Birmingham, Joseph Chamberlain grew up in London. He was born at Camberwell on 8 July 1836, the first of nine children in the family of Joseph senior and his wife Caroline (nee Harben). When he was ten the family moved to Highbury where Joseph attended a school in Canonbury Square before completing his formal education at University College School between 1850 and 1852.

The Chamberlains were of solid, commercial stock with a business in the City of London since the early eighteenth century. They had prospered first as cordwainers but later as boot and shoe wholesalers and it was in the family firm that Chamberlain began his working life at the age of sixteen. Though he had excelled at school his father was unwilling to finance a university education, fearing that he would not be able to offer the same advantage to all his sons.

Chamberlain's Birmingham connection dates from 1854 when he was sent to represent the family's interest in the woodscrew manufacturing business established by his uncle, John Sutton Nettlefold. He applied himself assiduously as the firm expanded, proving especially adept at marketing and sales. Unlike many British manufacturers of the period Chamberlain was attentive to the precise requirements of foreign customers. A ruthless, competitive instinct was also much in evidence as Nettlefold and Chamberlain built up a near-monopoly share in the market for machine-made screws. When the Chamberlain family interest was sold to the Nettlefolds in 1873 Joseph's share realised £120,000. His financial independence secured, he was now free to concentrate on politics.

His political career had already begun. As Unitarians the family were rooted in the radical tradition of English nonconformity. It was fitting, therefore, that Chamberlain was drawn into politics through the Birmingham (later National) Education League after 1867. Not only was he able to champion the radical cause of free, secular elementary education; he was also given ample opportunities to assail the Anglican establishment. As chairman of the League's executive, Chamberlain led the campaign to remove the guarantees underpinning Church schools in the 1870 Education Act. This brought him, for the first time, into conflict with Gladstone and the London-based leaders of official Liberalism.

In 1869 he had entered Birmingham politics as councillor for the St Paul's ward. Buttressed by Birmingham's Liberal "Caucus", which maximised electoral suport, and by a sympathetic coterie of businessmen and nonconformist clergy, Chamberlain preached and practiced a municipal gospel which was to transform his adopted city. With Chamberlain as Mayor between 1873 and 1876 Birmingham became a byword for civic progress. Municipal enterprise abounded as gas and water supply were brought into public ownership and run profitably to the advantage of the city's ratepayers. Libraries, parks and other amenities were developed. More controversially, an ambitious improvement scheme covering 93 acres of the city centre was initiated. Insanitary slums gave way to New Street and Corporation Street, brick and mortar testimony to Chamberlain's radical vision. There was substance to the claim of an American observer in 1890 that

Birmingham was "the best-governed city in the world". Much of the credit for this lies with Chamberlain.

After unsuccessfully contesting Sheffield in 1874, Chamberlain entered parliament as a Liberal member for Birmingham at a by-election in 1876. He remained in the House of Commons for the rest of his life. Chamberlain's reputation as a radical preceded him and with Charles Dilke, with whom he formed a personal alliance, he was regarded as the most powerful radical contender for high office. When he formed the National Liberal Federation in 1877, thus providing himself with the capacity to disseminate Birmingham radicalism nationwide, it was clear to Gladstone and to Liberals of a Whiggish inclination that Chamberlain represented forces with which they would have to come to terms. After the Liberal victory at the 1880 general election Gladstone was obliged to recognise his claims. Less than four years after entering parliament Chamberlain achieved Cabinet rank as President of the Board of Trade.

His ministerial achievements at the Board were relatively modest. Though important legislation on bankruptcy and patents was steered through in 1883, Chamberlain's more radical attempt to impose safety obligations on shipowners in the interests of merchant seamen foundered in 1884. As Gladstone's government became embroiled in the complexities of Anglo-Irish relations and imperial policy it became especially important to maintain the impetus for reform. Chamberlain did not allow this to flag, campaigning in 1885 for his "Unauthorised Programme", a provocative restatement of the radical commitment to free education, land taxation and "three acres and a cow" for rural labourers. This was set in the context of the controversial doctrine of ransom. "What ransom", asked Chamberlain, "will property pay for the security it enjoys?"

Chamberlain's relationship with Gladstone was never comfortable but, when the point of departure arrived, it was Ireland, not the Unauthorised Programme, which was at issue. Despairing of pacification by other means, Gladstone sprang his home rule policy on the party in December 1885, just before the demise of Salisbury's short-lived government. Chamberlain was persuaded to take the Local Government Board in Gladstone's new administration, serving uneasily for a few weeks before resigning in March 1886, having failed to reach agreement with his leader. Though generally convinced that Ireland would benefit from good government rather than self government, Chamberlain was prepared to contemplate a federalist solution involving devolution for Wales, Scotland and Ireland (North and South) provided that the ultimate sovereignty of the Crown in Parliament remained intact. For Chamberlain, the exclusion of Irish representatives at Westminster, a feature of Gladstone's bill, was unacceptable. It signified separation and the first steps on a slippery slope leading to the break-up of empire.

At the second reading of the Home Rule Bill in June 1886 Chamberlain voted with the Opposition, effectively severing his connection with parliamentary Liberalism. Deserted by the National Liberal Federation, he found himself adrift and in strange company. Of the seventy-nine Liberal Unionists returned at the ensuing election, many were Whigs who had regarded Birmingham radicalism with disapproval. Haunted by cries of "Judas" which were to pursue him for the rest of his political career, Chamberlain explored the possibility of an alliance with Randolph Churchill, the self-appointed leader of "Tory Democracy" and then embarked on protracted negotiations with his former Liberal colleagues. When these failed at the Round Table Conference of 1887 the Liberal Unionists were drawn inexorably towards co-operation with the Conservatives, a process which accelerated after 1892 when Gladstone again placed home rule at the top of the political agenda. During this period Chamberlain's radicalism was rather muted though he did take up the cause of old age pensions after 1891.

When, in June 1895, Chamberlain accepted office under Lord Salisbury it seemed that he had cast off the mantle of his early radicalism. He had chosen to serve under a Prime Minister once derided as a representative of parasitic aristocracy, "those who toil not neither do they spin". Moreover, as Secretary of State for the Colonies, he had opted for a department which would constrain his interests in domestic social reform. It was, however, a decision consistent with his hawkish position on Egypt in 1882 and with his opposition to Irish home rule.

Chamberlain appears to have been determined to place both the Colonial Office and the "undeveloped estates" of the empire on a business footing. He was successful at Whitehall but there was little to show for his efforts elsewhere aside from some improvements arising from the recommendations of the Royal Commission on the West Indies in 1896. Above all he was anxious to promote imperial unity but his proposed "Zollverein" or customs union struck the rocks at the 1897 Colonial Conference and his tentative imperial preference scheme suffered the same fate in 1902.

The war in South Africa from 1899 to 1902 was, of course, a significant distraction from the pursuit of such long term aims. His Liberal opponents regarded it as "Chamberlain's war" in that his relentless brinkmanship after 1897, ostensibly on behalf of the "Uitlanders" in the Transvaal, had forced Kruger into a corner, leaving him no option but to fight. In addition, Chamberlain was also accused of pursuing an expansionist policy on behalf of Cecil Rhodes and other mining magnates who sought to wrap the Union Jack around their business interests. The origins of this charge may be traced to the Jameson Raid of 1895 and Chamberlain's economy with the truth regarding his own complicity at the subsequent enquiry. But if these events and the conduct of the war marked a less than glorious page in the history of the British Empire, Chamberlain retrieved some credit with his South African tour of 1902–1903 when his active diplomacy helped to reconcile British and Afrikaaner interests, laying the foundations for political union.

Chamberlain's turbulent career reached its final phase in May 1903 when he argued, in a speech at Birmingham, that Britain should abandon its long-established free trade policy. Initially his proposal involved the construction of a tariff which would serve to promote imperial unity by making it possible to offer remissions, or preferences, to the colonies. As the policy of tariff reform developed, however, the protective advantages likely to benefit hard-pressed British manufacturing industries were stressed. In addition, Chamberlain was persuaded, largely for reasons of electoral expediency, to suggest that the revenue derived from a tariff might be used to finance old age pensions or to reduce existing taxes on tea and sugar.

It was to no avail. Chamberlain failed to convince his Cabinet colleagues that tariff reform was practical politics and resigned in September 1903, thus freeing himself to campaign for what was, in effect, a new unauthorised programme. His crusade against Cobdenism between 1903 and 1905 backfired. Not only did he succeed in re-uniting the Liberal Party in defence of free trade but he also caused the Conservative and Liberal Unionist Parties to split into warring factions with disastrous consequences at the 1906 general election. Moreover, his arguments failed to persuade working class electors that their long-standing affection for the "large loaf" and the "free breakfast table" was misplaced. Food taxation, essential if meaningful preferences were to be given to empire producers, was an electoral liability. Though there was some consolation in that the "whole hog" tariff reformers predominated amongst the diminished Conservative and Liberal Unionist ranks in the 1906 parliament Chamberlain was not on hand to lead a revival. He suffered a stroke in July 1906 and remained an invalid, watching frustrated from the sidelines, until his death in July 1914.

Chamberlain was a radical and an imperialist. In the context of Liberal politics before 1886 it was natural that his radicalism should flourish, though it should be remembered that he had been, in Granville's phrase, "almost the biggest Jingo" in Gladstone's Cabinet of 1880. After 1886, in the context of Liberal Unionism, Chamberlain's imperialism predominated, though his support for pensions and workmens' compensation suggest that the radical flame continued to flicker. At no point, however, was he able to blend his two preoccupations into a harmonious theme, a failure which ensured that Chamberlainite politics were persistently volatile and likely to test conventional party ties to breaking point. This set limits to what he was able to achieve but left him at the epicentre of the convulsions which shook the British political system in the late nineteenth and early twentieth centuries. "Joe", as Winston Churchill observed, "was the one who made the weather".

Chapter Two

Chronology

1836	3 July born at 3 Camberwell Grove, London.
1844–1846	Educated at a school in Camberwell run by Miss Charlotte Pace and her sister Harriet.
1846	Family moves to number 25 Highbury Place. Joseph attends the Reverend Arthur Johnson's school in Canonbury Square.
1850	Attends London University College School.
1852	Enters his father's shoemaking business at 36 Milk Street, London. Joseph teaches at a Sunday school supported by his local Unitarian chapel at Little Carter Lane, Doctor's Common, near St Paul's, until 1854. He attends science lectures at the Polytechnic.
1854	Enters firm of Nettlefold, a screw manufacturing company in Birmingham. Nettlefold becomes Nettlefold and Chamberlain with Joseph's father providing the capital to buy machines capable of making screws mechanically.
1854–1867	Joseph prospers with Nettlefold and Chamberlain, who expand by taking over many small workshops producing woodscrews in Birmingham.

1861	Joseph marries Miss Harriet Kenrick.
1862	Birth of Chamberlain's first daughter, Beatrice.
1863	Birth of son, Austen. Death of Harriet.
1865	Joseph joins the Birmingham Liberal Association.
1867	Establishment of the Education League in Birmingham. Soon afterwards this becomes the National Education League. It advocates compulsory free and universal education.
1868	The Birmingham Liberals develop the 'caucus' system. Chamberlain marries Miss Florence Kenrick, cousin of his late wife.
1869	Joseph Chamberlain joins the National Educational League. He is elected to the Town Council; birth of his second son, Neville.
1870	Chamberlain becomes chairman of the National Education League. Birth of his second daughter, Ida.
1870–1873	Chamberlain is at the forefront of the Nonconformist campaign against the Forster Education Act of 1870.
1872	Birth of Chamberlain's third daughter, Hilda.
1873–1876	In November 1873 Chamberlain is elected Mayor of Birmingham. He is re-elected twice, in 1874 and 1875. With the Birmingham Liberal machine behind him he embarks on a programme of urban reconstruction. Arguing that "all regulated monopolies should be controlled by representatives of the people and not left in the hands of private speculators" he organises the municipal takeover of the local gas and water industries. In 1875 an Improvement Scheme for the centre of Birmingham is introduced, clearing slums and creating Corporation Street.
1874	Chamberlain stands for the Liberal cause as a Parliamentary candidate in the General Election, for the constituency of Sheffield. He loses to J.A. Roebuck, the sitting tenant. In the same year he retires from his business commitments to concentrate on full-time politics.
1875	Death of the second Mrs Chamberlain in childbirth.

1876 In June Chamberlain resigns as Mayor. He is elected unopposed to Parliament as the M.P. for Birmingham.

1877 Chamberlain is central to the creation of the National Liberal Federation, an extension of the Birmingham caucus principal to national politics.

1880 Chamberlain is re-elected to Parliament at the General Election. He enters the Cabinet of W.E. Gladstone, now forming his second administration, as President of the Board of Trade. He moves to Highbury in Birmingham.

1883 In February Chamberlain introduces the Bankruptcy and Patent Rolls Bills. In March he speaks out against the House of Lords. In November he calls for universal manhood suffrage and for equality of treatment for Ireland.

1884 In January Chamberlain fails to pass the Merchant Shipping Bill. More attacks on the House of Lords follow in March, along with calls for a Franchise Bill. This is passed in December (although it falls short of Chamberlain's demands).

1885 Chamberlain speaks out in favour of land reform in January. He calls for agricultural workers to be given their own plots of land. In May Chamberlain brings proposals for a sweeping reform of local government in Ireland in front of the Cabinet. They are designed to provide autonomy for the Irish through the establishment of a 'central board' or 'Irish Board', an elected body with full powers over education, land and communications. The Cabinet rejects the scheme. The government falls in June. A caretaker administration is formed under Lord Salisbury. Chamberlain introduces the "unauthorised programme" in an attempt to capture the Liberal Party for the Radical cause. There is a General Election at the end of the year. The Liberals win with a majority of 86 over the Conservatives, 86 Parnellites holding the balance.

1886 Formation of Gladstone's Third Ministry in February. Chamberlain is appointed President of the Local Government Board. In March he resigns out of disagreement on principle with Gladstone's commitment to Home Rule for Ireland. Chamberlain inaugurates the National Radical Union in June. Gladstone's government falls on the issue of Home Rule and Lord Salisbury becomes Prime Minister in August.

1887–1888 Chamberlain becomes an official delegate at the Washington Fisheries Conference.

1888 In April Chamberlain becomes President of the Liberal Unionist Association. In November he marries Miss Mary Endicott, whom he had met while in the United States.

1891 In May Chamberlain writes "Favourable Aspects of State Socialism" for *The North American Review.*

1892 In February Chamberlain writes "Old Age Pensions" for the *National Review.* There is a General Election in July, won by the Liberals. Gladstone forms his fourth administration.

1894 Gladstone resigns after his failure to pass a Home Rule Bill. Lord Rosebery becomes Prime Minister in March. In September Chamberlain argues that Conservatives and Radicals share common ground in support for social reform.

1895 The Rosebery administration falls in June. A caretaker government composed of Conservatives and Liberal Unionists is formed under Lord Salisbsury. Chamberlain is appointed Colonial Secretary. In December there is a General Election. Salisbury is returned as Prime Minister at the head of a Unionist coalition. Chamberlain stays at the Colonial Office. Start of the Anglo-American Venezuela border dispute.

1895–1896 At the end of December and the start of January the Jameson Raid takes place.

1896 Chamberlain sets up a Royal Commission to investigate the causes of poverty and unemployment in the West Indies. Resolution of the Venezuela dispute after personal negotiations by Chamberlain with Richard Olney, the U.S. Secretary of State.

1897 Sir Alfred Milner is appointed High Commissioner for South Africa in March. The report of the Royal Commission is followed by economic and diplomatic measures designed to support the West Indian sugar industry. A Select Committee of the House of Commons established to investigate allegations that Chamberlain colluded in the Jameson Raid.

He is exonerated. In September Chamberlain backs the use of armed force on the part of Sir George Goldie to expel the French from north-west Nigeria. Chamberlain presides over a Colonial Conference and advocates an Imperial federation. He helps to steer the Workmen's Compensation Bill through the House of Commons.

1898 In August a preferential tariff is introduced for British imports into Canada. Throughout this year and into 1899 there is growing antagonism between the British government and the Boer Republics over the issue of rights for the Uitlanders. Partition of West Africa between the British, French and Germans. Chamberlain attempts, unsuccessfully, to negotiate an Anglo-German alliance. He announces a five year plan for the reconstruction of the West Indies.

1899 Chamberlain organises Treasury and private financial support for the establishment of a Department of Tropical Medicine and for the London and Liverpool Schools of Tropical Medicine. His attempts during this year to negotiate a settlement between Britain and the Boer republics fail. The Boer War breaks out in October. Chamberlain unsuccessfully presses for the expenditure of a £222 million dividend from Britain's Suez Canal shares on Colonial development schemes.

1900 Chamberlain introduces the Australian Commonwealth Bill in May. Also in May, the University of Birmingham, to whose establishment Chamberlain had been central both as driving force and as mobiliser of financial support, receives its Royal Charter.

1901 In January Chamberlain chairs the first meeting of the Court of Governors of Birmingham University.

1902 The Boer War ends on 31 May. Chamberlain leaves Britain for a tour of South Africa in November. Introduction of the 1902 Education Bill, designed to establish a national system of primary, secondary and technical schools, thus abolishing the School Boards established under the Forster Act, many of which are by now controlled by Nonconformists. Chamberlain swallows his Nonconformist misgivings and argues in favour of the Bill. Introduction of a corn duty to help to pay for the war. At the July Colonial Conference Chamberlain argues that the corn duty could become the basis for a system of Imperial preference. In the same month Salisbury resigns and is replaced by Arthur Balfour.

1903 Chamberlain returns to the United Kingdom from South Africa in March. Repeal of the corn duty. In May Chamberlain argues for tariff reform, based on Imperial preference, to create greater Imperial unity, safeguard British industry and to finance social reforms. The Unionists split into 'free fooders' and supporters of Chamberlain's proposals, who form a national organization, the Tariff Reform League, in July. Chamberlain opens the tariff reform campaign in October, at Glasgow. Balfour replies by arguing only for reciprocity. Establishment of the Tariff Commission, to make the case for a 'scientific tariff'.

1904–1906 Chamberlain campaigns relentlessly to convert the Unionists to tariff reform, using the League to exercise grass-roots pressure on MPs. The Unionists, completely divided, suffer a series of by-election defeats.

1906 The Balfour government is trounced by the Liberals at the polls in January. By July Chamberlain is poised to take over the Unionist Party but suffers a stroke which paralyses him on one side. Day to day leadership of the Campaign is taken over by his son Austen and ill-health compels Joseph's retirement from public speaking.

1909 Balfour commits the Unionists to support for Tariff Reform.

1910 There are two General Elections. The Unionists lose both (although by no means as badly as in 1906) to the Liberals.

1911 Chamberlain makes his last appearance in the House of Commons, to be sworn in after the Election.

1913 The Unionists revolt against the commitment to food taxes. Their new leader, Andrew Bonar Law, abandons them.

1914 Death of Joseph Chamberlain on 3 July.

Chapter Three

Manuscript and Archival Sources

A. THE CHAMBERLAIN ARCHIVE, MANUSCRIPTS AND RARE BOOKS READING ROOM, UNIVERSITY OF BIRMINGHAM MAIN LIBRARY

1. JC: Youth and Family Matters
This collection includes correspondence with mother and sisters; details of Joseph's marriage settlements; Joseph's notebook relating to affairs of Nettleford and Chamberlain.

2. JC2:JC2/1–2/2. Board of Trade, 1880–1885
There are two volumes of papers, consisting of letters and documents relating to, for example, merchant shipping, seamen's compensation, bankruptcy and the reorganisation of the commercial and statistical department.

3. JC3:JC3/1–3/5. Washington Fisheries Conference, 1887–1888
There are 3 volumes of papers. Mostly they comprise Chamberlain's correspondence with the Foreign Office, Salisbury,

and with the other participants in the Fisheries Conference. The third volume contains printed papers, comprising the text of the Treaty and related documents.

4. JC4. Press Cuttings, 1868–1914
The Chamberlain Press File is the subject of a separate essay in this bibliography. See chapter 11.

5. JC5:JC5/1–5/76.
Chamberlain's correspondence with those whose political careers became intertwined with his. The largest collection is with John Morley. Letters from Dilke, Salisbury and Harcourt also figure. Subjects discussed range from local matters (for example, local politics and the establishment of Birmingham University) to party politics and to national issues such as education, Ireland, South Africa and tariff reform. The section as a whole is very large and runs to 26 volumes, with 76 files in all.

6. JC6:JC6/1–6/6. Domestic Politics
A large selection of papers concerning Chamberlain's domestic political preoccupations from his time as a local politician to his years as a Cabinet Minister. Subject matter includes education, employer's liability, old age pensions, poor relief, agrarian questions and Liberal and Liberal Unionist Party affairs. JC6/5 includes notebooks on 1880 franchise agitation on the Scottish land question, and on the 1885 land campaign. There are 6 volumes in all.

7. JC7:JC7/1–JC7/5. Foreign Affairs
There are 5 volumes in all. They consist mostly of official papers and private correspondence relating to, for example, the occupation of Egypt; the Afghan frontier; Anglo-German and Anglo-American relations; the Venezuela dispute and the Fashoda incident, 1898.

8. JC8:JC8/1–8/10
I. JC8/1–8/2 contain Chamberlain's personal jottings, in diary common placebook, and in the form of a long memorandum

on political events, 1880–92. This last document almost amounts to a political autobiography and details Chamberlain's Parliamentary and Cabinet career, his breach with the Liberals over Home Rule for Ireland and the establishment of the Liberal Unionists. These files contain other material of interest, notably extracts from the diary of Sir Charles Dilke, 1880–85.

II. JC8/3–JC8/10. The subject matter throughout these files is Ireland. Papers include Chamberlain's proposals for local government reform and public works, his split with the Gladstonians over Home Rule and correspondence with leading participants in the Irish crisis. There is an exhaustive set of memoranda and correspondence as well as a selection of newspaper articles and pamphlets relating to Chamberlain and Home Rule. The documents show Chamberlain's willingness to consider radical measures in Ireland as long as they stopped short of dissolving the Union. A separate file (JC8/6/1–2) also contains Chamberlain's Home Rule Notebooks, 1886–1893, which contain brief records of the Parliamentary proceedings relating to the Irish question.

9. JC9:JC9/1–9/7. Imperial Affairs, both personal and official. Contains memoranda, correspondence and some pamphlets relating to Imperial affairs, mostly between 1879 and 1900. There are 7 files, covering areas such as India, South Africa, Australia, Canada, Gibraltar, Hong Kong and West Africa. Issues raised include the Niger negotiations, Colonial conflicts in West Africa, railway development, Canadian government reform, Fashoda and slavery in Zanzibar.

10. JC10:JC10/1–JC10/5. South Africa
I. JC10/1–2 mainly concern the Jameson Raid (December 1895–January 1896) and the subsequent inquiry. JC10/3 contains printed documents about the raid including Chamberlain's telegraphed correspondence with Hely-Hutchinson and Robinson. The material in this volume and in JC10/4–10/5 also relate to the tension between HMG and the Transvaal

Republic, centring on treatment of the Uitlanders, which led to war in 1899.

II. JC10/6–JC10/9.
These volumes contain Chamberlain's correspondence relating to the Jameson Raid and the South African Crisis, with the leading personalities involved such as Rhodes, Hely-Hutchinson and Milner. There is also material concerning Chamberlain's dealings, as Colonial Secretary, with the British South Africa Company. This covers the background to and consequences of the Jameson Raid, and the proposed extension of the Bechuanaland railway to take in Tanganyika.

11. JC11:JC11/1–JC11/39.
These files contain Chamberlain's general correspondence, 1900–1902. There are letters to and from Lord Salisbury, A.J. Balfour, Lord Balfour of Burleigh, C.T. Ritchie, Queen Victoria, King Edward VII and other significant political figures of the time. The most commonly occurring subjects are the Boer War, its origins and development, and education. Taxation policy and colonial issues outside South Africa are also discussed.

12. JC12. Miscellaneous
These papers relate to Chamberlain's work in helping to found the University of Birmingham, his interest in the possibility of creating a Jewish homeland in East Africa and his concern to advance research into tropical diseases. There is also a substantial file of press cuttings about, mostly, Chamberlain's journey to South Africa, 1902–1903.

13. JC13:JC13/1–13/2.
All the papers here relate to South Africa, 1900–1903. Most are letters to and from Lord Milner concerning the Boer War, but there are also memoranda, notes and Colonial Office Minutes.

14. JC14:JC14/1–14/4.
These documents deal exclusively with colonial matters,

1900–1902, other than South Africa. A good deal of the material concerns the standard of living and the possibilities of development in the West Indies, and the question of sugar duties—which Chamberlain favoured. There is also a collection of Cabinet prints and papers relating to miscellaneous affairs but above all to South Africa.

15. JC15:JC15/1–15/456. Canada
An extensive collection (photocopies) of correspondence between Chamberlain and Canadian politicians such as Laurier. There is a very large file of letters between Chamberlain and Lord Minto (Governor-General). The rest of the material concerns for the most part commercial negotiations between Canada and Belgium.

16. JC16:JC16/1–16/7.
JC16/1–16/2 contain essays, respectively, on "John Milton" (1864) and on "Popular Delusions" (1869); JC16/3 has statistical material used by Chamberlain for speeches and articles in favour of tariff reform. JC16/4–16/6 are volumes of correspondence with contemporary politicians (e.g. Hicks-Beach) and with Queen Victoria (typewritten, with some duplication of material with JC5/71, JC11/37 and JC11/12). JC16/7 is concerned with overseas trade.

17. JC17:JC17/1–17/6.
Most of the contents of JC17 concern imperial commercial relations and the Colonial Conference of 1902. There is some material, also, relating to Cuba in 1902–1903.

18. JC18:JC18/1–18/20.
These papers form a miscellaneous collection covering matters as diverse as imperial defence, the future of Canada, the Baghdad railway, the Cabinet Crisis of 1903, Chamberlain's resignation and fiscal policy.

19. JC19:JC19/1–19/7.
A collection of correspondence relating to colonial and imperial issues, to tariff reform and to the affairs of the Liberal

Unionist Association. JC19/3/1 is a report on the Basin of the Upper Nile, Egypt.

20. JC20:JC20/1–20/4.
These files contain miscellaneous correspondence. A small amount relates to South African affairs in 1905; most of the rest concern the subject of preferences, the Canadian Tariff Commission, tariff reform and the Unionist Party in 1905.

21. JC21:JC21/1–21/2.
These files contain a miscellany of correspondence, most of it about tariff reform and the 1906 election. There is a file comprising letters between Chamberlain and L.S. Amery, 1905-10 (JC21/1/1–21).

22. JC22:JC22/1–22/158. Miscellaneous correspondence, 1907–1914.
Subjects range from tariff reform, the 1910 elections and home rule to Chamberlain's health and retirement, announced in 1914.

23. JC23:JC23/1–23/5.
Most of this file is comprised of diary extracts and letters by Mary Chamberlain, 1901–1914, and of press cuttings and miscellaneous correspondence about Joseph in 1913 and 1914 and after his death. The file also contains Joseph's will.

24. JC24:JC24/1–24/4.
This file contains a few press cuttings about Chamberlain, dating from his centenary in 1936. The rest relates to Garvin's biography, comprising a notebook, letters and a typed synopsis.

25. JC25:JC25/1–25/4.
A miscellany of press cuttings and biographical proofs for the *Encyclopaedia Britannica* relating to a variety of famous 19th and 20th century politicians. The papers also contain newspaper material about Birmingham (1928–1929) and a history of South Africa, illustrated, published in 1913 and written in Afrikaans and English.

26. JC26:JC26/1–26/19.
A small file containing a few early letters by Joseph Chamberlain. Most of this relates to Birmingham politics of the 1860s.

27. JC27:JC27/1–27/141.
This file consists of photocopies of Chamberlain (mainly Austen) and Garvin material—mostly correspondence—in the University of Texas Library.

28. JC28:JC28A and JC28B.
This file comprises the correspondence between Joseph and Mary Chamberlain (nee Endicott) from their courtship until the end of Joseph's life. The letters deal almost exclusively with personal and private matters. JC28A is Joseph's letters to Mary; JC28B vice versa.

29. JC29. Joseph Chamberlain: Letters Additional.
There are 486 entries. These are letters to and from Chamberlain filed separately from the main collection because they were obtained outside the Chamberlain family. Correspondents are drawn from Chamberlain's business associates, family and political colleagues at local and national level. In all but two cases the letters span the period 1860–1914. The exceptions are dated 1941 and relate to the acquisition of Chamberlain's correspondence by the University.

30. *Joseph Chamberlain: Unpublished Ministerial Papers.*
The vast bulk of these are kept in the University of Birmingham. Ministerial minutes, memoranda and correspondence can, however, also be found in the archives of the departments presided over by Chamberlain, namely the Board of Trade (1880–1885), Board of Local Government (1885-1886), and Colonial Office (1895-1903), kept at the Public Record Office, Kew, London (see chapter 3, section E).

There are no special Ministerial deposits for Chamberlain; the papers are broken up according to subject. However, official correspondence and a register of correspondence concerning, specifically, Chamberlain's tour of South Africa while he was Secretary of State for the Colonies is held at C.O. 529 and C.O. 638.

B. DEPOSITS OF JOSEPH CHAMBERLAIN'S PAPERS OUTSIDE THE UNIVERSITY OF BIRMINGHAM

31. Joseph Chamberlain MSS (misc)
Notebook relating to the purchase and working of the Birmingham Gas Undertaking, 1870–1879. A photostat reproduction is held in the Birmingham Collection at Birmingham Central Library (accession no. 415186).

32. Joseph Chamberlain MSS (misc)
The Archives Department at Birmingham Central Library holds a small collection of Chamberlain letters at MS135. These are mainly unimportant items deriving from his duties as Mayor but there is an interesting letter to George Baker on foreign policy, dated from May 1878, and a letter to H.W. Wilson on the use of statistics in the tariff reform campaign, dating from July 1903.

33. Transcript of Joseph Chamberlain's Notebook kept at Nettlefold and Chamberlain, Broad Street, Birmingham, 1866–1874, continued up to 1884 by his successors.
Transcript (typed) made in 1964 L F62/2, accession no. 743678, Birmingham Central Library. Thirty three foolscap pages of typed entries from Chamberlain's notebook, mainly recording routine dealings with clients, etc., and providing a valuable insight into his business methods.

C. PUBLISHED COMPILATIONS OF ORIGINAL PAPERS

34. Boyd, C.W. (ed.). *Mr Chamberlain's Speeches* London, 1914.
A two volume selection which provides representative coverage of all phases of Chamberlain's political career.

35. Chamberlain, Joseph. *Foreign and Colonial Speeches* London, 1897.
An indexed collection of twenty speeches by Chamberlain from the period 1887-1897 in which Chamberlain explores various imperial themes. Edited anonymously.

36. Chamberlain, Joseph. *A Political Memoir 1880–1892* (edited from the original manuscript by C.H.D. Howard) London, 1953.
An important document, described by the editor as "Chamberlain's defence . . . against the charges brought against him" during the period of the home rule crisis, the Liberal schism and the failure of reunion.

37. Grinter, Robin. *Joseph Chamberlain: Democratic Unionist and Imperialist* London, 1971.
A representative collection of speeches and documents by Chamberlain covering all the stages of his political career, this is designed for use in secondary schools.

38. Howard, C.H.D. "Documents Relating to the Irish 'Central Board' Scheme, 1884–1885", *Irish Historical Studies* 8 (1952–1953), 237–263.
A selection of documents concerning Chamberlain's 'central board' or 'national councils' scheme, in order to supplement those on the same issue printed in Garvin's *Life of Joseph Chamberlain.*

39. Microfilm Publications.
There are at the time of writing (January 1994) no microfilm publications relating to the papers of Joseph Chamberlain.

D. UNPUBLISHED PAPERS OF PERSONS CLOSELY ASSOCIATED WITH JOSEPH CHAMBERLAIN

i. Family Papers in the Manuscript Reading Room, University of Birmingham

Joseph Chamberlain: Documents (Unpublished) Relating to Him in the Papers of Austen Chamberlain

40. AC1/4:AC1/4/1–1/4/5/53
This is a miscellaneous collection. It contains family documents (for example Joseph's birth certificate) and letters from Joseph to Austen and Beatrice, which touch on political as

well as family matters. JC1/4/2/1–64 consists of Joseph's notes for speeches, mostly concerning preference.

41. AC1/6:AC1/6/1–1/7/5/11, AC1/7
Most of the material here comprises family memorabilia, photographs and press cuttings (for example about the 70th birthday celebrations in Birmingham in 1906). One curiosity is a play written by Chamberlain called "Politics, a Political Comedy".

Joseph Chamberlain: Unpublished Material Concerning Him in the Papers of Neville Chamberlain

42. NC1/6/1–1/6/110
These papers contain family documents, some miscellaneous pictorial material relating to Joseph; a memoir of Joseph written by Neville for his children and correspondence between father and son (most of which concerns the Andros sisal growing scheme), up to and including 1914.

Joseph Chamberlain: Unpublished Papers Concerning Him in the Archives of Beatrice, Ida and Hilda Chamberlain

43. BC 3/3/1–28
This is a collection of letters from Joseph to Beatrice between 1875 and 1900. Some provide Joseph's accounts of visits in Britain and overseas; the rest deal with family affairs. There is no political content.

44. BC 4/1/1–6
Joseph Chamberlain to Hilda Chamberlain, 1888–1892. These letters are concerned exclusively with domestic affairs and family news.

45. BC 5/1–5/2/3
A collection of photographs, contemporary political material and documents relating to Joseph Chamberlain. An edition of *The Searchlight of Greater Birmingham* (13 November 1913)

is included, as is the programme of the annual meeting of the Tariff Reform League, 7 July 1905.

46. BC 5/2a/1
A memoir by Joseph about his second wife, to her children, 5 April 1875.

47. BC 5/3
This is a large fragment of an account, in Ida Chamberlain's handwriting, of the South African crisis. The manuscript runs, from pp.97–203. It is accompanied by a typed copy of ten and a half pages of the manuscript. It is unlikely that Ida is the author, but provenance is at present (January 1994) unknown.

48. BC5 4/1–23
A collection of press cuttings, pamphlets, cards and letters, mostly relating to Joseph Chamberlain's career in politics. There are a few family and social memorabilia from early days, for example programmes of amateur theatricals in which Joseph was involved.

49. BC 5/5/1
"The Labour Question"—reprint of an article by Joseph published in November 1892 edition of *The Nineteenth Century*.

50. BC 5/10/3–5/10/5
Hilda Chamberlain's memoirs of her father (Joseph). Includes the typescript of a broadcast talk on 15 September 1953.

ii. Political Contacts

NRA numbers refer to the reports filed at the National Registry of Archives, Quality House, Quality Court, London, WC2A 1HP. Researchers seeking material located in British public archives will find it useful to consult J. Gibson and P. Peskett, *Record Offices: How to Find Them* (4th ed., Birmingham 1988), published by the Federation of Family History Societies.

51. Balfour MSS
Arthur James Balfour served as Chief Secretary for Ireland

between 1887 and 1891, Leader of the House of Commons and First Lord of the Treasury between 1891 and 1892 and again between 1895 and 1905. He was Prime Minister from 1902 to 1905 and continued to lead the Conservative Party until 1911. Thus Chamberlain served with him under Salisbury after 1895 and under him until September 1903. Even after Chamberlain's resignation his relationship with Balfour was crucial as the Conservative leader struggled to find a middle way between the 'whole-hog' tariff reformers and the free fooders.

The main body of Arthur Balfour's papers are held in the Department of Manuscripts at the British Library, Great Russell Street, London, WC1B 3DG. Two substantial boxes of letters from Chamberlain, spanning the years 1887–1900 and 1901–1911 are located at Ad.MSS 49773 and 49774.

Some additional Balfour papers are held at the Scottish Record Office, H.M. General Register House, Princes Street, Edinburgh, EH1 3YY. These contain letters from Chamberlain about parliamentary tactics in the late 1880s and 1890s and some correspondence on colonial affairs from 1898–1900. This collection also includes the papers of Gerald Balfour who served as President of the Board of Trade from 1900 to 1905. Some letters from Chamberlain about tariffs are to be found amongst his miscellaneous political correspondence. (NRA 10026).

52. Bell MSS

Chamberlain's letters to Charles Frederick Moberley Bell, manager of *The Times*, are held by the Record Office of News International. The correspondence dates from the period 1900–1904 and is mainly concerned with tariff reform. (NRA 19359).

53. Bonar Law MSS

Law's papers, held at the House of Lords Record Office, London, SW1A 0PW, include about thirty items, mostly letters relating to Chamberlain dating from the period after 1906 when illness had forced him onto the fringes of political life. Law, who was to become leader of the Conservative Party in 1911, was very much a tariff reformer at the time. (NRA 19286).

54. Bright MSS
The veteran Anti Corn Law League campaigner served as a Liberal M.P. for Birmingham from 1857 to 1885 and, again, for Central Birmingham from 1885 to 1889; he served briefly with Chamberlain under Gladstone while holding the office of Chancellor of the Duchy of Lancaster from 1880 to 1882. Chamberlain's letters to John Bright dating from 1875 to 1888 are located at Ad.MSS 43387 in the Department of Manuscripts, British Library, Great Russell Street, London, WC1B 3DG.

55. Churchill MSS
Lord Randolph Churchill's papers, held at the Churchill Archives Centre, Churchill College, Cambridge, CB3 0DS, include fifty-six letters from Chamberlain dating from the mid to late 1880s, mainly on Irish home rule and party politics in the aftermath of the Liberal schism. Winston Churchill later made reference to this correspondence and the fleeting possibility of a political alliance between 'Radical Joe' and the architect of 'Tory Democracy' after 1886 (see Julian Amery, *The Life of Joseph Chamberlain*, iv, 275). (NRA 13273).

56. Croft MSS
Henry Page Croft was a youthful enthusiast for imperial preference and his papers at the Churchill Archives Centre, Churchill College, Cambridge, CB3 0DS, include, at CH 15-18, some items related to tariff reform campaign in the period 1903–1913. (NRA 15709).

57. Deakin MSS
Alfred Deakin, Prime Minister of Australia in 1903–1904, 1905–1908 and 1909–1910, was sympathetic to Chamberlain's imperial preference policy. Twenty-five items, mainly

letters from Chamberlain dating from 1903–1905, are amongst Deakin's papers held in the Manuscripts Section, National Library of Australia, Canberra. (NRA 25702).

58. Devonshire MSS
Chamberlain's relationship with Lord Hartington, later the Eighth Duke of Devonshire, generated correspondence which provides an essential source for the history of Liberal Unionism. Devonshire, after Chamberlain himself, was the most significant figure in the Liberal Unionist Party after 1886, serving as Chairman of the Liberal Unionist Council until ousted by a tariff reformers' coup in 1904. He served in the Cabinet with Chamberlain from 1895, resigning at the same time, but for different reasons, in controversial circumstances in 1903.

The Duke's papers, held by the Librarian, Chatsworth House, Chatsworth, Derbyshire, contain a substantial and important collection of letters from Chamberlain spanning the years 1877–1904. The material is especially rich for the years 1886–1887, 1894–1895 and 1903–1904, reflecting the preoccupation with home rule and then tariff reform. (NRA 20594/16).

59. Dilke MSS
Chamberlain's intimacy with Sir Charles Wentworth Dilke, his fellow radical of the 1870s and early 1880s, is reflected in a substantial correspondence covering the period 1871 to 1906. The letters are especially numerous for the period 1883–1885 when both held posts in Gladstone's administration. The Dilke MSS are located at Ad.MSS 43885-43889 at the Department of Manuscripts, British Library, Great Russell Street, London, WC1B 3DG.

60. Escott MSS
Sixty letters from Chamberlain to T.H.S. Escott, editor of the important Liberal journal, the *Fortnightly Review*, are to be found amongst Escott's papers at Ad.MSS 58777 in the Department of Manuscripts, British Library, Great Russell

Street, London, WC1B 3DG. They date from 1882–1886 and are concerned with Escott's conduct of the *Review*, Chamberlain's contributions and Liberal politics in general. (NRA 16926).

61. Fiedler/Harding MSS
Located in the Special Collections Department, The University Library, The University of Birmingham, Edgbaston, Birmingham, B15 2TT, this archive contains a few letters from Chamberlain which date from 1898–1902 and indicate his views on teaching modern languages at the new Birmingham University. (NRA 13793).

62. Garvin MSS
The papers of James Louis Garvin, political journalist and Chamberlain's first official biographer, include letters from Chamberlain dating from 1877 to the end of his active career in 1906. Some letters to W.T. Stead are found in this collection and also letters from Austen Chamberlain written on behalf of his father between 1908 and 1914. Garvin's papers include some later material relating to the first three volumes of the official Chamberlain biography. The Garvin MSS are held by the Humanities Research Library, The Library, The University of Texas, Austin, Texas 78712. Copies of this material are to be found amongst Chamberlain's own papers at Birmingham University Library, reference JC27/1–141.

63. Gladstone MSS
Chamberlain's letters to Gladstone constitute a major primary source for the history of the Liberal Party in the late nineteenth century. They cover all important aspects of Liberal politics over the years 1873 to 1893 and are especially important in connection with the Irish home rule crisis of 1886 and the subsequent party schism. Researchers will find this material located at Ad.MSS 44125 and 44126 in the Department of Manuscripts, British Library, Great Russell Street, London, WC1B 3DG.

64. Green MSS

Three letters from Chamberlain to Alice Stopford Green, Irish nationalist and widow of the historian J.R. Green, are to be found at reference MS15074 in the National Library of Ireland, Kildare Street, Dublin, 2. The most important, dated May 1902, relates to prisoners in the West Indies.

65. Halsbury MSS

The First Earl of Halsbury, Lord Chancellor from 1895 to 1905, served with Chamberlain under both Salisbury and Balfour. His papers, located at Ad.MSS 56367–56377, in the Department of Manuscripts, British Library, Great Russell Street, London, WC1B 3DG, contain eighteen letters from Chamberlain from the years 1890–1905 and some additional letters from Mary and Austen. (NRA 6238).

66. Hamilton MSS

Edward Hamilton was Gladstone's private secretary from 1880 to 1885 while Chamberlain served in the Cabinet as President of the Board of Trade. The collection of his papers at Ad.MSS 48623–48624 in the Department of Manuscripts, British Library, Great Russell Street, London, WC1B 3DG, contain a number of Chamberlain's letters from 1881 to 1884, supplementing material in the Gladstone MSS.

67. Harcourt MSS

The papers of Sir William Harcourt are held in the Department of Western MSS, Bodleian Library, Oxford, OX1 3BG. They contain, at reference MS Harcourt dep. 59–61, Chamberlain's contribution to a substantial correspondence ranging across the years 1870–1902. Harcourt served, as Home Secretary, with Chamberlain under Gladstone from 1880–1885 but the most significant concentration of material dates from 1887 and the thwarted discussions about Liberal reunion. There are also some letters from Chamberlain to Lewis Harcourt from the years 1894–1906. (NRA 3679).

68. Hewins MSS
William Albert Samuel Hewins, economist and economic historian, was the Director of the London School of Economics before taking up appointment as Secretary of Chamberlain's unofficial Tariff Commission in 1904. He was Chamberlain's principal economic adviser during the tariff reform campaign. His papers are held at the University Library, University of Sheffield, Western Bank, Sheffield, S10 2TN, and contain some Chamberlain letters from 1903–1906 and other items of tariff reform interest.

69. Hicks-Beach MSS
Sir Michael Hicks-Beach, the First Earl St. Aldwyn, was Chancellor of the Exchequer under Salisbury from 1895–1902 and thus had the main responsibility for funding "Chamberlain's War". Chamberlain's letters to his Cabinet colleague are principally concerned with colonial and Boer War issues. They are located amongst Hicks-Beach's papers, reference PCC 86, at Gloucestershsire Record Office, Clarence Row, Alvin Street, Gloucester, GL1 3DW. (NRA 3526).

70. Kimberley MSS
The National Registry of Archives reports some Chamberlain correspondence with John Woodhouse, First Earl of Kimberley, who served as Secretary of State for India in Gladstone's Cabinet from 1882–1886. Kimberley's papers were reported to be in the possession of his family and inaccessible to researchers but inquiries can be directed to Norfolk Record Office, Central Library, Norwich, NR2 1NJ. (NRA 1274).

71. Lister Institute MSS
Chamberlain's correspondence with the British Institute for Preventive Medicine concerns the supply of anti-plague serum and dates from initiatives on tropical diseases undertaken during his period at the Colonial Office. This small collection of letters forms part of the archive of the Lister Institute and is held at the Contemporary Medical Archives Centre, Well-

come Institute for the History of Medicine, 183 Euston Road, London, NW1 2BN. (NRA 29786).

72. Lloyd MSS
George Lloyd, Lord Lloyd of Dolobran, was a youthful convert to tariff reform. The Lloyd MSS at the Churchill Archives Centre, Churchill College, Cambridge, CB3 0DS, contain, at reference GLLD 18/14, a small collection of letters and telegrams from Chamberlain and others on the subject of tariffs dating from 1903–1914. (NRA 12663).

73. Lloyd Family MSS
The papers of the Lloyd family in the Archives Department, Birmingham Central Library, Chamberlain Square, Birmingham, B3 3HQ, include, at reference MS 488/10–14, five letters from Chamberlain to Councillor Felix Hadley. These date from 1875–1877 and are mainly concerned with Birmingham parks.

74. Lugard MSS
Chamberlain's connection with Frederick Lugard, Baron Lugard of Abinger, date from his Colonial Office days. Chamberlain ordered Lugard to Nigeria in 1895, appointing him Commissioner in 1897 and charging him with the responsibility of maintaining the upper hand against the French in West Africa. Lugard's papers at Rhodes House Library, Rhodes House, South Parks Road, Oxford, OX1 3RG, are in two sections: MSS Brit. Emp. and MSS Lugard. Letters from Chamberlain and other relevant material are found in both sections. Under MSS Brit. Emp. there is correspondence, notably at S54, S59 and S62, relating to Lugard's work in Bechuanaland, Uganda and Nigeria. Under MSS Lugard 2/6, there is a bound volume of letters from Chamberlain, dating mainly from 1895–1903; and at 9/7 there is some correspondence about a projected Chamberlain memorial. (NRA 8555).

75. Lyttleton MSS
A small collection of letters from Chamberlain spanning the

years 1899–1905 are to be found in the papers of Oliver Lyttleton, First Viscount Chandos, at the Churchill Archives Centre, Churchill College, Cambridge, CB3 0DS. (NRA 19700).

76. Maxse (Frederick) MSS
Chamberlain's correspondence with the journalist Frederick Maxse ranges over a variety of political topics from 1872 to 1894. There is also a substantial file of letters relating to inquiries made by Chamberlain about the French taxation system in 1880–1881. The originals are held at West Sussex Record Office, County Hall, Chichester, PO19 1RN. Copies are located at references U1599.C5/1 and C5/2 in the Cecil-Maxse MSS held at the Kent Archives Office, County Hall, Maidstone, ME14 1XQ. (NRA 10619, 20659).

77. Maxse (Leopold) MSS
Leo Maxse's papers at the West Sussex Record Office, County Hall, Chichester, PO19 1RN, reflect his interests as a staunch imperialist and advanced tariff reformer. As editor of the *National Review* he corresponded with Chamberlain as well as with Leo Amery and other members of the advanced guard of the tariff reform movement. This substantial collection is open to researchers but permission must be sought and received from the owners of the Maxse papers. (NRA 10619).

78. Midleton MSS
As St. John Brodrick, the First Earl of Midleton served as Secretary of State for War between 1900 and 1903. His papers, held at the Brenthurst Library, Box 87184, Houghton, 2041 South Africa, contain thirty-three letters from Chamberlain regarding the political and military conduct of the South African War in 1901 and 1902.

79. Milner MSS
The papers of Alfred, First Viscount Milner, are held at the Department of Western MSS, Bodleian Library, Oxford, OX1 3BG. They are important for an understanding of Chamber-

lain's South African policy from 1897, when Milner was appointed Governor of Cape Colony, to 1903. As High Commissioner for South Africa from 1897 Milner was very much Chamberlain's 'man on the spot' as Britain's relationship with the Boers deteriorated. Official Chamberlain-Milner correspondence, mainly printed, is at MSS Milner dep. 166–168; private correspondence is at dep. 170–171. Papers concerning Chamberlain's visit to South Africa in 1902–1903 are at dep. 237, fos. 1–110. (NRA 14300).

80. Minto MSS
The Fourth Earl of Minto served as Governor General of Canada from 1898 to 1904 and engaged in a "personal and semi-official" correspondence with Chamberlain while he remained at the Colonial Office. The correspondence is important for an understanding of Anglo-Canadian relations at the turn of the century. Chamberlain's letters to Minto are in the Eliot-Murray-Kynynmond MSS held by the Department of Manuscripts, National Library of Scotland, George IV Bridge, Edinburgh, EH1 1EW. (NRA 10476).

81. Monk Bretton MSS
John William Dobson, Second Baron Monk Bretton, was Chamberlain's private secretary at the Colonial Office between 1900 and 1903. His papers are deposited at the Department of Western Manuscripts, Bodleian Library, Oxford, OX1 3BG. They form a substantial collection, mainly comprising Colonial Office memoranda in which South African affairs from 1895, the conduct of the war, arrangements for Chamberlain's South Africa tour and the Colonial Conference of 1902 feature prominently. Some private correspondence between Chamberlain and Monk Bretton is located at box 82 (D). Box 86, containing miscellaneous Colonial Office material from 1895 onwards, was passed to Monk Bretton by his predecessor, Lord Ampthill.

82. Mundella MSS
Chamberlain's connection with A.J. Mundella, Liberal M.P.

for Sheffield from 1868 to 1885, dates from his own unsuccessful campaign in Sheffield at the general election of 1874. Mundella's papers are deposited at the University of Sheffield Library, Western Bank, Sheffield, S10 2TN. They contain a small number of letters from Chamberlain spanning the period 1877–1885, useful for insights into his early radicalism. (NRA 6510).

83. National Liberal Club MSS
The National Liberal Club archive is at the University of Bristol Library, Tyndall Avenue, Bristol, BS8 1TJ. It includes fifteen letters from Chamberlain to Alfred Austin, written between 1887 and 1906, concerning politics and contributions to the *National Review.* (NRA 33764).

84. Newhailes MSS
Sir Charles Dalrymple was Conservative M.P. for Ipswich from 1886 to 1906. His papers, held by the Department of Manuscripts, National Library of Scotland, George IV Bridge, Edinburgh, EH1 1EW, contain some letters from both Joseph and Mary Chamberlain, written between 1896 and 1910. These are listed under "general correspondence" at 7228/232 (vii). (NRA 17690).

85. Northcote MSS
These include, at PRO 30/56, a small collection of letters from Chamberlain to Lord Northcote, Governor-General of Australia, between 1904 and 1908. They include interesting comment on the outcome of the 1906 general election and on Australian politics and are held by the Public Record Office, Ruskin Avenue, Kew, Richmond, Surrey, TW9 4DU. (NRA 23637).

86. Onslow MSS
The papers of the Fourth Earl are held at the Surrey Record Office, Guildford Muniment Room, Castle Arch, Guildford, GU1 3SX. They contain some personal and political letters from Chamberlain from the years 1896–1907, located mainly

at reference 173/7. Onslow served as Under Secretary of State for the Colonies from November 1900 to May 1903 during Chamberlain's time at the Colonial Office. (NRA 1088).

87. Passfield MSS
Beatrice Potter (later Webb) was courted unsuccessfully by Chamberlain after the death of his second wife. Some Chamberlain letters from the years 1883–1887 are amongst her papers held at the British Library of Political and Economic Science, 10 Portugal Street, London, WC2A 2HD. (NRA 7533, 28876).

88. Pembroke MSS
Some letters from Chamberlain to Sidney Herbert, Fourteenth Earl of Pembroke, dating from 1890–1912, are reported amongst the Herbert family papers held in the Muniment Room at Wilton House. Inquiries should be directed to the Wiltshire Record Office, County Hall, Trowbridge, Wiltshire, BA14 8JG. (NRA 22080).

89. Playfair MSS
Some Chamberlain letters from 1894–1895 concerning the Royal Commission on the Aged Poor and from 1896 on the Venezuela dispute are amongst the First Baron Playfair's papers held at the Library of Imperial College of Science, Technology and Medicine, South Kensington, London, SW7 2AZ. (NRA 1156).

90. Rhodes MSS
Cecil Rhodes' papers are at Rhodes House Library, Rhodes House, South Parks Road, Oxford, OX1 3RG. Out letters and telegrams are at MSS Afr s 227. Some letters from Chamberlain survive at MSS Afr s 228. These concern the government of Cape Colony, C27/53(11); the extension of the Bechuanaland Railway, C18/8 and the Cape to Cairo Railway project, C27/100(4). Some important material relating to Chamberlain and the Jameson Raid inquiry is contained in correspondence between W.T. Stead and Rhodes' solicitor,

Hawkesley, at C11/1–13; further correspondence from 1897 on this episode is at C27/74(5).

91. Ridley (Blagdon) MSS
The papers of the Second Viscount Ridley are held at the Northumberland Record Office, Melton Park, North Gosforth, Newcastle-upon-Tyne, NE3 5QX. Ridley was the first Chairman of the Tariff Reform League and ZRI 25/99 contains a useful bundle of correspondence on tariffs and some letters from Chamberlain. (NRA 4468).

92. Salisbury MSS
Access to the papers of Robert Arthur Talbot Gascoyne-Cecil, the Third Marquess of Salisbury, Prime Minister in 1885–1886, 1886–1892 and 1895–1902, is restricted to scholars working at postgraduate level and above. Applications for access should be made in writing to the Librarian and Archivist, Hatfield House, Hatfield, Hertfordshire, AL9 5NF. The papers contain approximately 215 letters from Chamberlain across the period 1887–1902 as the Liberal Unionists moved into an alliance with the Conservatives allowing Chamberlain to take his seat in Salisbury's Cabinet after 1895.

93. Sandars MSS
As Arthur Balfour's private secretary, Sandars was frequently in correspondence with Chamberlain, especially during the period of Balfour's premiership from 1902 to 1905. The extensive collection of his papers at the Department of Western Manuscripts, Bodleian Library, Oxford, OX1 3BG, contain letters from Chamberlain for the period 1891–1906 and, also, some Chamberlain-Balfour correspondence for 1893–1904. This material is very important for Conservative and Liberal Unionist high politics in the late nineteenth and early twentieth centuries and is located at MSS Eng. Hist., c. 724–7752. (NRA 19043).

94. Selborne MSS
An extensive body of political letters covering the main issues

of the periods 1888–1897 and 1898–1911 respectively is located at MS Selborne 8 and 9 in the Department of Western Manuscripts, Bodleian Library, Oxford, OX1 3BG. Selborne was the Chief Whip of the Liberal Unionist Party between 1895 and 1900, later serving alongside Chamberlain in Balfour's government. (NRA 17810).

95. Sladen MSS
The NRA listing records one letter from Chamberlain in Douglas Sladen's "envelope book" for 1896–1904. The novelist's papers are to be found at the Central Library, Little Green, Richmond, Surrey, TW9 1QL. (NRA 14252).

96. Smith of Jordanhill MSS
Parker Smith, M.P. for Partick, served as Chamberlain's Parliamentary Private Secretary between 1902 and 1906. His papers, held at the Strathclyde Regional Archives, P.O. Box 27, City Chambers, Glasgow, G2 1DU, are an important source for the tariff reform campaign. Chamberlain's letters, at reference TD1/116, provide a running commentary on its progress. (NRA 20864).

97. Stanhope of Chevening MSS
Edward Stanhope served under Salisbury as President of the Board of Trade, Colonial Secretary and Secretary of State for War in rapid succession between 1885 and 1892. His papers at the Kent Archives Office, County Hall, Maidstone, ME14 1XQ, include a file of letters from Chamberlain on general political topics in the period 1884–1891, the years of the Liberal schism and the Liberal Unionist drift towards an arrangement with the Conservatives. (NRA 25095).

98. Strachey MSS
J. St. Loe Strachey edited the *Cornhill Magazine* in 1896–1897 and, thereafter, the *Spectator*. Amongst his papers at the House of Lords Record Office, London, SW1A 0PW, are about twenty Chamberlain items from the years 1887–1900, including letters on social, foreign and colonial policy. Stra-

chey's papers for the period after 1903 are useful for tracing the history of the Unionist Free Fooders who opposed Chamberlain's tariff policy. (NRA 19285).

99. Tariff Commission MSS
Chamberlain's unofficial Tariff Commission was established under the direction of Professor Hewins in 1904. It gathered evidence on the state of agriculture and industry with a view to the construction of a "scientific" tariff. Its archive is a valuable source for the economic historian if used with an awareness of its political bias. There are some letters from Chamberlain, notably at reference TC6 8/1 and 8/2, about the Commission and its work. The Commission's papers are held by the British Library of Political and Economic Science, 10 Portugal Street, London, WC2A 2HD. (NRA 25116).

100. Tariff Reform League MSS
Unfortunately very little League material has survived. The Modern Records Centre, University of Warwick Library, Coventry, CV4 7AL, does hold a run of the League's journal, *Monthly Notes on Tariff Reform*, at MSS 223. This was acquired with material from the Empire Industries Association which has some claim to be regarded as the League's successor body.

101. Wilson MSS
A Liberal M.P. of radical persuasion, H.J. Wilson's links with Chamberlain arose principally from the general election of 1874, see especially reference M.A. 5924–5926. Chamberlain maintained contact after his unsuccessful campaign at Sheffield and there are some additional letters on Liberal politics dating from 1876–1878 at M.D. 2588. Wilson's papers are held at the Central Library, Surrey Street, Sheffield, S1 1XZ. (NRA 7902).

102. Wrightson MSS
Sir Thomas Wrightson's papers are held by Sir Mark Wrightson at Neasham Hall, Croft, Darlington, Co. Durham. As an

ironmaster and Conservative M.P., Wrightson leaned towards protectionism. Fourteen letters from Chamberlain, written between 1899 and 1906, survive, mainly on tariffs and associated political issues. Researchers should make inquiries through Durham County Record Office, County Hall, Durham, DH1 5UL. (NRA 15949).

E. MATERIAL CONCERNING JOSEPH CHAMBERLAIN HELD IN THE PUBLIC RECORD OFFICE, KEW, LONDON

Joseph Chamberlain held three Cabinet posts during his career. He served twice under Gladstone as President of the Board of Trade between April 1880 and June 1885 and, briefly, as President of the Local Government Board in February and March 1886. As Liberal Unionist leader he claimed his place as Secretary of State for the Colonies in June 1895 serving continuously under Salisbury and Balfour until his resignation in September 1903. Files held at the Public Record Office at Kew, London, relate to the business of the ministries which Chamberlain headed. Researchers are advised to consult the relevant sections of the *Public Record Office Current Guide*, Part I, for a detailed classification of departmental papers. Board of Trade papers are listed in section 601 of the *Current Guide*, Local Government Board papers are in section 410 and Colonial Office papers are in section 803. Researchers may also wish to consult papers relating to Chamberlain's work at the Washington Fisheries Conference in 1887–88 which are located in the Foreign Office files. It is stressed that these files contain, in general, business correspondence of the departments concerned rather than material generated by Chamberlain himself.

Board of Trade. Formal minutes of the Board for the years 1880 to 1885 are located at reference BT5/88–93 but these relate principally to staffing and other establishment matters. During Chamberlain's tenure the most significant change in the work of the Board was caused by the Bankruptcy Act of 1883 and this is reflected in the files relating to the newly established Bankruptcy Department at BT37/1–2. A useful impression of the range of responsibilities undertaken by the Board under Chamberlain may be gained from perusing BT13/11–13 and BT15/16–25.

Local Government Board. Chamberlain's brief stay at the Local Government Board was not without significance in the development of unemployment policy. A few days before leaving office he issued the so-called "Chamberlain Circular" of 15 March 1886 encouraging poor law guardians to provide relief work for unemployed artisans. Board circulars are located at reference MH10. Useful information on the status and work of the Board in the late nineteenth century is on file at MH78/44.

Colonial Office. The Colonial Office files represent the full range of work undertaken by this department. The material is arranged in classes relating to particular colonies and these are specified in the *Current Guide* at section 803.9.1. The general business correspondence of the department for the years 1895 to 1903 is located at CO323/400–490. Registers of correspondence for these years are at CO378/13–16. Scholars interested in the details of Chamberlain's tour of South Africa after the Boer War can find material at CO529 and CO638. Those wishing to explore the early history of Anglo-Australian relations will find some papers under PRO 30/56. These are letters from Chamberlain to Lord Northcote, Governor-General of Australia, 1904–1908. For the most part they concern the issues of tariffs and imperial preference. Chamberlain's personal papers and the papers of Lord Monk Bretton at the Bodleian Library are likely to be more useful to researchers interested in Chamberlain's involvement in imperial affairs.

Foreign Office. FO301/9 is a box of manuscript and printed materials relating to the work which Chamberlain undertook as leader of the British delegation at the Washington Fisheries Conference. It includes a copy of a personal letter from Salisbury, dated 2 March 1888, indicating that the ensuing treaty owed much to the manner in which Chamberlain had conducted the delicate negotiations.

F. PUBLISHED PAPERS OF ASSOCIATES

103. Barnes, John and Nicolson, David (eds.). *The Leo Amery Diaries* Volume I, 1896–1929. London, 1980.
References to Chamberlain, in the form of letters from him and meetings with him, are scattered rather thinly across the diaries. Most of the entries concern tariff reform.

104. Blumenfeld, R.D. *R.D.B.'s Diary 1887–1914* London, 1930.
Extracts from the diaries of the well-connected editor of the *Daily Express*. An intriguing entry for 24 December 1901 attributes anti free trade remarks to Chamberlain; see 23 June 1903 for Chamberlain and the origins of the Tariff Reform League.

105. Headlam, Cecil (ed.). *The Milner Papers* Volume I, South Africa, 1897–1899; Volume II, South Africa, 1899–1905. London, 1931, 1933.
Students of Chamberlain's South Africa policy during his time as Colonial Secretary will find these two volumes very useful.

106. Matthew, H.C.G. (ed.). *The Gladstone Diaries* Volumes IX-XI, 1874–1886. Oxford, 1987–1990.
Most of the entries concerning Chamberlain can be found in volumes X and XI. In the main they take the form of letters to Chamberlain from Gladstone which express the latter's concern at Chamberlain's views and activities ranging from advanced radicalism to oposition to home rule. Unsurprisingly the Irish question occupies increasing space but there is also some room for mention of Chamberlain's activities as President of the Board of Trade, 1880–1885 and President of the Local Government Board, 1885–1886.

At the time of writing (January 1994) the *Gladstone Diaries* have reached the end of 1886.

107. Skelton, Oliver Douglas. *Life and Letters of Sir Wilfred Laurier* 2 vols., Oxford, 1922.
Canada's Prime Minister after 1896 endured a difficult rela-

tionship with Chamberlain and the British government. Chapters XI and XV of volume II provide details with reference to the Colonial Conferences of 1897 and 1902 and preferential trade.

108. Stephens, P. and Saywell, J.T. (eds.). *Lord Minto's Canadian Papers: A Selection of the Public and Private Papers of the Fourth Earl of Minto*, Volume I, 1898–1900, Toronto, 1981; Volume II, 1900–1904, Toronto, 1983.

Minto was Governor General of Canada from 1898 to 1904. These volumes include all his correspondence with Chamberlain over this period. Volume I is especially of interest for the Canadian contribution to the Boer War; volume II reflects the growing importance of preferential trade as a political issue.

G. PARLIAMENTARY PAPERS CONCERNING JOSEPH CHAMBERLAIN

109. Chamberlain's speeches for the period of his life in Parliament can be found in the appropriate volumes of *Hansard*.

110. Aberdare Commission on the Aged Poor. Report of the Royal Commission on the Aged Poor (Chairman, Lord Aberdare), c. 7684 H.C. (1895), xiv, 1; minutes of evidence, c. 7684–I-II H.C. (1895), xiv, 123, and xv, 1.
During these proceedings Chamberlain reveals his enthusiasm for old age pensions, accepting that it might be necessary to introduce a tax on corn to finance them—an early sign of the views which led him to call for tariff reform in 1903.

111. Chamberlain Committee on Small Holdings. Report from the Select Committee on Small Holdings (Chairman, Joseph Chamberlain), H.C. 313 (1889) xii, 1. Further report, H.C. 223 (1890), xvii, 183.
Proceedings of a parliamentary committee presided over by Chamberlain, established to investigate the feasibility and desirability of providing small-holdings for working class

people—a cause for which Chamberlain had been and was to remain an enthusiast.

112. Jackson Committee on the Jameson Raid. Special Report from the Select Committee on British South Africa (Chairman, W.L. Jackson), H.C. 64 (1897), ix, 1. Second report, H.C. 311 (1897), ix, 5. Appendices H.C. 311–I (1897), ix, 607. Papers of the select committee on British South Africa concerning its investigation into the Jameson Raid fiasco. Chamberlain, accused of complicity, is cross-questioned and issues a robust statement and memorandum in self-defence.

Chapter Four

Personal Writings

A. ARTICLES, PAMPHLETS AND SPEECHES

113. Chamberlain, Joseph. Volume of Articles by Joseph Chamberlain.
Twenty two published articles from the period 1873–1905 at C1/8/1–22. Birmingham University Library.

114. Chamberlain, Joseph. "A Bill for the Weakening of Great Britain", Nineteenth Century xxxiii (April 1893), 545–588.
Chamberlain's arguments against Gladstone's second Home Rule Bill. Ulster's position under Home Rule discussed at some length.

115. Chamberlain, Joseph. "The Case Against Home Rule. No. XII—From a Liberal Unionist Point of View", *Pall Mall Gazette* (8 August 1893)
Vehemently expressed opposition to the second Home Rule Bill, including some tub-thumping at the expense of the Irish Nationalists.

116. Chamberlain, Joseph. "The Caucus", *Fortnightly Review* xxx N.S. (November 1878), 721–741.
Original version of this article. See next item.

117. Chamberlain, Joseph. "The Caucus", National Federation of Liberal Associations, Birmingham, 1878.
The Caucus defended as increasing "the influence of the people in the management of their own affairs". Reprinted from the *Fortnightly Review*. This edition contains a footnote commenting on the resolution of W.E. Forster's difficulties with the Liberal Party in Bradford.

118. Chamberlain, Joseph. "The Caucus; and A New Political Organisation", National Liberal Federation, Birmingham, 1880.
Chamberlain's important articles from the *Fortnightly Review* republished in one volume.

119. Chamberlain, Joseph. "The Educational Policy of the Government from a Nonconformist Point of View: Paper Read at the Suffolk Nonconformist Conference on April 3rd, 1872", National Education League, Birmingham, 1872.
Chamberlain argues that the religious education of schoolchildren lies outside the proper sphere of state intervention.

120. Chamberlain, Joseph. "Favourable Aspects of State Socialism", *North American Review* no. 152 (May 1891), 534–548.
Indicates the benefits which have followed the extension of government functions and argues for a continuation of this process.

121. Chamberlain, Joseph. "Free Schools", *Fortnightly Review* xxi N.S. (January 1877), 54–72.
Chamberlain argues for the state funding of education; "free schools are a necessary corollary of compulsion".

122. Chamberlain, Joseph. "The Home Rule Campaign", *National Review* xxiii (May 1894), 305–318.

The history of the campaign is reviewed and its prospects bleakly assessed in the light of Gladstone's recent retirement.

123. Chamberlain, Joseph. *Imperial Union and Tariff Reform: Speeches Delivered from May 15 to November 4, 1903* London, 1903.
Chamberlain's introduction, dated 9 November 1903, explains that he has modified "a few expressions . . . to which exception has been taken".

124. Chamberlain, Joseph. "The Labour Question", *Nineteenth Century* xxxii (November 1892), 677–710.
The Labour movement astutely analysed: Chamberlain indicates a social reform programme designed to secure working class support for the Unionists.

125. Chamberlain, Joseph. "Labourers and Artisans' Dwellings", *Fortnightly Review* xxxiv N.S., no. cciv (December 1883), 761–776.
Argues that the case for housing improvement is urgent and that the cost should fall largely on the landowners.

126. Chamberlain, Joseph. *Land Nationalisation: A Criticism on Recent Treaties by Mr H. George and Mr A.R. Wallace.M. Two short articles reprinted from the Pall Mall Gazette* 24 and 29 January 1882 and published as a pamphlet.

127. Chamberlain, Joseph. "The Liberal Party and Its Leaders", *Fortnightly Review* xiv N.S., no. lxxxi (1 September 1873), 287–302.
The party leaders attacked for their lack of Liberal convictions; advocates "Free Church, Free Land, Free Schools, and Free Labour".

128. Chamberlain, Joseph. "Manufacture of Iron Wood Screws", in Timmins, A. (ed.), *The Resources, Products and Industrial History of Birmingham and the Midlands Hardware District* London, 1866, 604–709.

A succinct account of the development of wood screw manufacture reflecting on the recent growth of factory production.

129. Chamberlain, Joseph. "Municipal Government—Past, Present, and Future", *New Review* 10, no. 61 (June 1894), 649–661.
Article reviewing sympathetically the operation of municipal institutions and outlining four principles to ensure that good local government continues.

130. Chamberlain, Joseph. "Municipal Institutions in America and England", *The Forum* (November 1892), 267–281.
A comparative study notable for Chamberlain's explanation of the legitimate functions of municipal government on pp. 280–281.

131. Chamberlain, Joseph. "Municipal Public Houses", *Fortnightly Review* xxi N.S., no. cxxii (February 1877), 147–149.
Chamberlain defends the Birmingham proposals for public-house reform against various critics, notably Robert Lowe.

132. Chamberlain, Joseph. "Nelson's Year and National Duty", *The Outlook* (11 March 1905).
An impassioned plea for imperial preference as the first step towards imperial union. "Commercial union has in other cases preceded political organisation". Also published as a separate pamphlet by the Imperial Tariff Committee, Birmingham.

133. Chamberlain, Joseph. *The New Democracy: Its Wants, Its Claims, and Its Rights* Birmingham, 1885.
Pamphlet containing Chamberlain's speeches at Birmingham and Ipswich in January 1885 which outlined the doctrine of "ransom".

134. Chamberlain, Joseph. "A New Political Organisation", *Fortnightly Review* xxviii N.S. (1 July 1877), 126–134.
The Birmingham Liberal Caucus described and defended with some comments on Gladstone's recent visit to the city.

135. Chamberlain, Joseph. *A New Political Organisation* Birmingham, 1877.
Article reprinted from the *Fortnightly Review*. See item no. 135.

136. Chamberlain, Joseph. "The Next Page of the Liberal Programme", *Fortnightly Review* xiv N.S., no. xciv (1 October 1874), 405–429.
In the aftermath of Liberal defeat at the 1874 General Election Chamberlain urges moderates to move towards the radicals.

137. Chamberlain, Joseph. "Old Age Pensions", *National Review* xviii (February 1892), 721–739.
An interim summary of conclusions reached by a voluntary commons committee on pensions provides a framework for Chamberlain's own views.

138. Chamberlain, Joseph. "Old Age Pensions and Friendly Societies", *National Review* xxiv (January 1895), 592–615.
A revised and enlarged version of his speech at Birmingham on 6 December 1894.

139. Chamberlain, Joseph. *Patriotism.* Address delivered to the students of the University of Glasgow on 3 November 1897, on the occasion of his installation as Lord Rector, Westminster, 1897.
Chamberlain claims to have "consistently sought . . . the greatness of the Empire and the true welfare of the people at large".

140. Chamberlain, Joseph, and Loch, C.S. *Pauperism and Old Age Pensions* London, 1892.
Pamphlet containing Chamberlain's letter to Loch of the Charity Organisation Society, 26 November 1891, and Loch's lengthy reply. (Originally published in the *Times*, 28 January 1892).

141. Chamberlain, Joseph. *The Radical Platform: Speeches by the Rt. Hon. J. Chamberlain, M.P.* Edinburgh and London, 1885.

Labelled "Authorized Edition", this contains Chamberlain's speeches at Hull, Warrington, Glasgow and Inverness in August and September 1885.

142. Chamberlain, Joseph. "A Radical View of the Irish Crisis", *Fortnightly Review* xlv N.S. (February 1886), 273–284.
Chamberlain argues that finding a solution to the Irish land question should take priority over Home Rule (signed "A Radical").

143. Chamberlain, Joseph. "The Right Method with the Publicans", *Fortnightly Review* xix N.S., no. cxiii (May 1876), 631–651.
In the interests of temperance, Chamberlain advocates permissive legislation empowering local authorities to acquire licenses.

144. Chamberlain, Joseph. "Shall We Americanise our Institutions?" *Nineteenth Century* xxviii, no. 166 (December 1890), 861–875.
Argues for changes in parliamentary procedures in order to combat filibustering and other obstructive tactics.

145. Chamberlain, Joseph. *Speeches on the Irish Question* London, 1890.
A collection of twenty speeches delivered between April 1887 and May 1890, published for the National Liberal Union.

146. Chamberlain, Joseph. "A Visit to Lapland, with Notes on Swedish Licensing", *Fortnightly Review* xx N.S., no. cxx (December 1876), 691–708.
Chamberlain's favourable impressions of the "Gothenberg system" where public-houses were managed on behalf of the municipality.

147. Lucy, H.W. (ed.) *Speeches of the Right Hon. Joseph Chamberlain, M.P., with A Sketch of His Life* London, 1885.
A collection of twenty-six speeches from 1881–1885 with a brief, sympathetic biographical introduction.

B. PREFACES FOR PAMPHLETS AND BOOKS WRITTEN BY POLITICAL ALLIES AND ASSOCIATES

148. Croft, Henry Page. *The Path of Empire* London, 1912.
Chamberlain's preface, dated 20 January 1912, provides a sympathetic overture to Croft's imperialist tract.

149. Cunningham, William. *The Case Against Free Trade* London, 1911.
A critique of free trade with particular reference to the imperial theme by an eminent historical economist, with a preface by Joseph Chamberlain, dated 14 June 1911, giving his view of "the imperial problem today".

150. Garvin, J.L. *Imperial Reciprocity: A Study of Fiscal Policy* 2nd edition. London, 1903.
A collection of pro-tariff articles, reprinted from the *Daily Telegraph*, prefaced by a letter from Chamberlain, mainly on the subject of food taxes.

151. Garvin, J.L. *Tariff or Budget: The Nation and the Crisis* London, 1909.
Two page preface by Chamberlain, dated 14 December 1909, urges electors to vote for tariffs and against constitutional reform.

152. Gould, E.R.L. *Popular Control of the Liquor Traffic* London, 1894.
Published for the Public House Reform Association; Chamberlain's introduction, dated 13 December 1894, advocates the Gothenberg system.

153. Impey, Frederick. *Three Acres and A Cow* London, 1885.
Chamberlain's preface, dated December 1885, restates "unauthorised" Liberal policy on local government reform and allotments for agricultural labourers. Impey is described as secretary of the Allotments and Small Holdings Association.

154. *The Radical Programme* London, 1885.
Chamberlain's preface describes the text as an attempt to provide "a definite and practical Programme for the Radical Party".

155. *Unionist Policy for Ireland* London, 1888.
Articles from the *Birmingham Post* explaining Liberal Unionist policy with a substantial preface by Chamberlain, dated September 1888. Published under the auspices of the National Radical Union.

156. Vince, C.A. *Mr Chamberlain's Proposals: What They Mean and What We Shall Gain By Them* London, 1903.
The secretary of the Imperial Tariff Committee makes the case for tariffs; includes a preface by Chamberlain dated 24 September 1903.

Chapter Five

Biographies

157. Amery, Julian. *The Life of Joseph Chamberlain*, Volume IV, 1901–1903, At the Height of His Power. London, 1951.
The authorised "Life", begun by Garvin, was taken up by Amery and continued in the same fashion, drawing largely on the Chamberlain papers. This volume provides sympathetic coverage of the end of the Boer War and the origin of the tariff reform policy.

158. Amery, Julian. *The Life of Joseph Chamberlain*, Volume V, 1901–1903, Joseph Chamberlain and the Tariff Reform Campaign. London, 1969.
Publication of the authorised biography continued after a break of eighteen years but, essentially, in the same fashion. Volume V incorporates some material from volume IV and continues the account up to Chamberlain's departure from the Cabinet in September 1903.

159. Amery, Julian. *The Life of Joseph Chamberlain* Volume VI, 1903–1968. London, 1969.

Amery's concluding volume follows Chamberlain through the last years of active political life. Three chapters discuss the legacy of Chamberlain's tariff reform and imperial preference policy and its fate in the years after 1914.

160. Amery, L.S. "Joseph Chamberlain".
Transcript of a talk broadcast on the B.B.C. Midland Service, 1 August 1952; useful on Chamberlain as a public speaker.

161. Botwood, H.A. "Mr. Chamberlain in Caricature: A Biography in Cartoon", Birmingham, 1901.
Four articles attributed by Birmingham Central Library to Botwood and taken from the *Birmingham Daily Mail*. Unfortunately they are not illustrated. The second in the series is notable for an interview with F. Carruthers Gould on "why he caricatures the Member for West Birmingham".

162. Bradley, Isaac. "Joseph Chamberlain", *Central Literary Magazine*, XI, no. 8 (October 1914), 300–311.
A useful obituary article from a Birmingham perspective concludes that Chamberlain was "a truer liberal" than many who reproached him.

163. Churchill, Winston S. "Joseph Chamberlain" in *Great Contemporaries* London, 1937.
An elegant biographical essay combining a significant overview of Chamberlain's political career with astute insights into his personality; essential and stimulating reading.

164. Creswicke, Louis. *The Life of the Right Honorable Joseph Chamberlain* London, 1904.
A monumental four volume biography sympathetic towards Chamberlain which quotes extensively from his speeches. Volume I covers his career to 1885; volume II to 1895; volume III to 1902 and volume IV deals largely with his South African tour of 1902–1903 and the early stages of the tariff campaign.

165. Egerton, Hugh Edward. "Chamberlain, Joseph", in *Dictionary of National Biography: Twentieth Century 1912–21* Oxford, 1927.
A sympathetic account of Chamberlain's life, concentrating on his political career.

166. Elletson, D.H. *The Chamberlains* London, 1966.
Joe, Austen, Neville, their wives and children are the subject of this rather overawed family biography; an essentially narrative approach.

167. Fraser, Peter. *Joseph Chamberlain, Radicalism and Empire, 1868–1914* London, 1966.
Sophisticated political biography drawing heavily on the recently available Chamberlain papers; contains interesting chapter on his relationship with Beatrice Webb.

168. Gardiner, A.G. "Joseph Chamberlain" in *Pillars of Society* London, 1913, 38–49.
An eminent liberal journalist provides a brilliant but bleak assessment of Chamberlain's career. "It is a tale for tears".

169. Garvin, J.L. *The Life of Joseph Chamberlain* Volume I, 1836–1885, Chamberlain and Democracy. London, 1932.
Substantial first volume of official biography based sympathetically on Chamberlain's papers. Garvin's objective is "to narrate the action and explain the motives".

170. Garvin, J.L. *The Life of Joseph Chamberlain* Volume II, 1885–1895, Disruption and Combat. London, 1933.
Garvin's second, important volume supplies the authorised version of Chamberlain's career in the turbulent period of the Liberal schism; he emerges unscathed from Garvin's account of the Crawford-Dilke divorce case and the downfall of Parnell.

171. Garvin, J.L. *The Life of Joseph Chamberlain* Volume III, 1895–1900, Empire and World Policy. London, 1934.
The authorised "life" continues with Garvin's account of

Chamberlain's years at the Colonial Office; absolves Chamberlain from complicity in the Jameson Raid.

172. Harries, F.J. *The Rt. Hon. Joseph Chamberlain: A Biographical Sketch* Pontypridd, 1913.
A sympathetic, sixteen page pamphlet biography which concludes by predicting the triumph of tariff reform at the next election.

173. Jay, Richard. *Joseph Chamberlain. A Political Study* Oxford, 1981.
Probably the least satisfactory recent major biography, redeemed somewhat by its "concluding essay"; contains a useful appendix on the Crawford-Dilke divorce case.

174. Jeyes, S.H. *Mr Chamberlain: His Life and Public Career* London, 1903.
An immense, detailed biography providing chronological coverage of Chamberlain's career to c. July 1903, with useful bibliographical appendices.

175. Jeyes, S.H. *Mr Chamberlain: His Life and Public Career* London, 1904.
Lavish, illustrated two-volume edition of Jeyes' 1903 biography with an additional chapter on the tariff reform agitation.

176. Jeyes, S.H. *The Right Hon. Joseph Chamberlain* London, 1896.
A full, sympathetic treatment of Chamberlain's political life with some prescient remarks on fiscal policy.

177. Judd, Denis, "Pioneers of the Welfare State. Radical Joe Chamberlain", *New Society* (28 October 1982), 165–167.
An appraisal of Joseph Chamberlain's political career. Chamberlain is depicted as a non-socialist radical whose belief that poverty could be erased by government action marked him as a founder of the welfare state.

178. Judd, Denis. *Radical Joe. A Life of Joseph Chamberlain* London, 1977.

A succinct and penetrating study of Chamberlain's persistent radicalism which argues that "his tactics were Fabian, his objectives essentially ameliorative".

179. Leech, H.J. *The Right Honorourable Joseph Chamberlain, M.P.: A Political Biography* Manchester, 1885.
A brief biography praising Chamberlain's radicalism and attacking his Liberal critics, notably Marriot.

180. Mackintosh, Alexander. *Joseph Chamberlain: An Honest Biography* London, 1906.
"Other modern statesmen have changed but none so completely". Mackintosh seeks an explanation for Chamberlain's apparent inconsistency.

181. Mackintosh, Alexander. *The Story of Mr Chamberlain's Life* London, 1914.
A competent biography published on Chamberlain's death which seeks to balance the apparent contradictions of his career.

182. Marris, N. Murrell. *Joseph Chamberlain: Imperialist 1836–1906* London, 1905.
A more partisan study supplementing Marris's earlier work: an appendix contains extracts from key speeches.

183. Marris, N. Murrell. *The Right Honourable Joseph Chamberlain, the Man and the Statesman* London, 1900.
A substantical and sympathetic volume outlining Chamberlain's life and career to 1900. Chamberlain's 1900 Election Address is appended.

184. Marsh, Peter. "Joseph Chamberlain", in *Dictionary of Business Biography* Volume 1, A-C. London, 1983, 643–648.
A succinct history of Chamberlain's career concentrating on his years in business with Nettlefold and Chamberlain, the Birmingham screw manufacturers. Chamberlain is revealed to have possessed acute commercial acumen.

185. Mee, Arthur. *Joseph Chamberlain: A Romance of Modern Politics* London, 1901.
Low-brow chronicle charting Chamberlain's rise from "a shoemaker's bench" to the Colonial Office.

186. Milner, Alfred (Vt), et al. *Life of Joseph Chamberlain* London, 1914.
Volume published on Chamberlain's death with contributions from Milner, Amery, Cox, Lucy, Macdonald and Spender. Milner writes on "Mr Chamberlain and Imperial Policy", 194–233.

187. Pedder, H.C. *The Right Hon. Joseph Chamberlain: A Study of His Creer as a Statesman* London, 1902.
A wordy and pseudo-scientific attempt to reveal "the animating purpose of a strong and interesting personality".

188. Petrie, Sir Charles. *The Chamberlain Tradition* London, 1938.
Gushing hagiography for the Right Book Club which has some curiosity value.

189. Powell, J. Enoch. *Joseph Chamberlain* London, 1977.
An intelligent political narrative enhanced by excellent illustrations which reveals as much about Powell as it does about his subject.

190. Rodgers, Edward,and Moyle, Edmund J. *Men of the Moment: No. 1 The Rt Hon Joseph Chamberlain* London, 1902.
A pamphlet biography in popular style published at the end of the Boer War and including astrological and phrenological perspectives.

191. Skottowe, B.C. *The Life of Joseph Chamberlain* Birmingham, 1885.
A brief, sympathetic biography by "a Birmingham man" written at the conclusion of the "unauthorised" campaign.

192. Vince, C.A. *Chamberlain Souvenir 1836–1906* Birmingham, 1906.

Illustrated brochure produced for Chamberlain's seventieth birthday celebrations and containing a brief eulogy by Vince.

193. Wallace, A. *The Right Hon. Joseph Chamberlain, M.P.* London, 1901.
This "bijou biography" provides a succinct overview of Chamberlain's career from a Conservative perspective.

194. W.T.T.D. "Joseph Chamberlain: In Memoriam", *Royal Botanic Gardens, Kew: Bulletin of Miscellaneous Information* no. 7 (1914), 233–236.
On Chamberlain the Orchid-grower and friend of Kew Gardens.

Chapter Six

Political Career

A. BIRMINGHAM RADICAL

i. The Birmingham Liberal Association and the Creation of the National Liberal Federation

195. Hanham, H.J. *Election and Party Management, Politics in the Time of Disraeli and Gladstone* London, 1959 and Hassocks, 1978.
An important chapter on the caucus concludes that Liberal associations were supplied with "an ideology and an organisational model", both "made in Birmingham".

196. Herrick, F.H. "The Origins of the National Liberal Federation", *Journal of Modern History* 17 (1945), 116–129.
Discusses how the caucus was established and reveals Gladstone's anxiety about the possibility that Liberal affairs might come under the direction of Birmingham and Chamberlain.

197. Tholfsen, Trygve R. "The Origins of the Birmingham Caucus", *Historical Journal* 2 (1959), 2, 161–184.

Argues that the real origins of the 1868 Birmingham Liberal caucus are to be found in Joseph Sturge's Complete Suffrage Union (founded 1842) and examines the political relationship between middle class Liberals and Birmingham artisans.

198. Watson, Robert Spence. *The National Liberal Federation from its Commencement to the General Election of 1906* London, 1907.
Watson, a Federation veteran, is especially scathing on those who followed Chamberlain in 1886, thus abandoning principles "once held dear and . . . so earnestly advocated".

ii. Chamberlain and the National Education League

199. Adelman, Paul. "Gladstone and Education 1870", *History Today* no. 1 (1970), 496–503.
This article discusses the impact on Liberal politics and ideology of the National Education League, formed in 1869 with Joseph Chamberlain in the chair.

200. Auspos, Patricia. "Radicalism, Pressure Groups and Party Politics: from the National Education League to the National Liberal Federation", *Journal of British Studies* 20, no. 1 (1980), 184–204.
Argues that the League represented a Chamberlainite vehicle for the advancement of broad-based radicalism; it was not merely a nonconformist pressure group.

201. Griffiths, Peter. "Pressure Groups and Parties in Late Victorian England. The National Education League", *Midland History* III, no. 3 (Spring 1976), 191–205.
Brief, scholarly and illuminating account of the League's work, 1867–1877, in which Chamberlain was prominent.

iii. Municipal Socialism

202. Briggs, Asa. *Victorian Cities* London, 1963.
The chapter on Birmingham's "civic gospel" provides an

excellent starting-point for a study of Chamberlain's 'age of improvement'.

203. Bunce, John Thackray. *History of the Corporation of Birmingham* Volume II. Birmingham, 1885.
Bunce's volume, "published for the corporation", covers the period 1852–1885 and provides a detailed chronicle of the improvements initiated under Chamberlain's leadership.

204. Hennock, E.P. *Fit and Proper Persons: Ideal and Reality in Nineteenth Century Urban Government* London 1973.
Contains a lucid and substantial study of local government in nineteenth century Birmingham; Chamberlain is seen as a "great entrepreneur in the public service".

205. Reigeluth, G.A. "Municipal Reform in Birmingham, England: 1873–1876". Johns Hopkins University, Ph.D. dissertation, 1981.
A study of the reform programme inaugurated by Chamberlain as Mayor of Birmingham. The thesis concentrates on the programme's impact on public health, concluding that its approach was imaginative, comprehensive and fiscally responsible.

iv. Parliamentary Candidate

206. Marsh, Peter T. " 'A Working Man's Representative': Joseph Chamberlain and the 1874 Election in Sheffield" in Bean, J.M.W. (ed.), *The Political Culture of Modern Britain: Studies in Memory of Stephen Koss* London, 1987, 56–74.
A succinct and penetrating account of Chamberlain's first foray as a parliamentary candidate: posing as a working man's representative, he is defeated by a combination of beer and the Bible.

B. PARLIAMENTARY CAREER, 1876–1886

i. Liberal M.P. and Cabinet Minister, 1876–1886

207. Barker, M. *Gladstone and Radicalism: The Reconstruction of Liberal Policy in Britain 1885–1894* Hassocks, 1975.

This is useful for its account of the rise of the National Liberal Federation and its analysis of the unauthorised programme.

208. Chamberlain, M.E. "Sir Charles Dilke and the British Intervention in Egypt, 1882: Decision Making in a Nineteenth Century Cabinet", *British Journal of International Studies* 13, no. 4 (1976), 227–235.
Discusses the role of the radicals, notably Dilke and Chamberlain, in the decision to intervene in Egypt, 1882.

209. Cooke, A.B., and Vincent, John. *The Governing Passion: Cabinet Government and Party Politics in Britain 1885–1886* Brighton, 1974.
Chamberlain's role is subjected to detailed scrutiny in both the "commentary" and "diary" section of this immensely scholarly but unwieldy volume.

210. Gwynn, Stephen, and Tuckwell, Gertrude. *The Life of the Rt. Hon. Sir Charles Dilke* London 1917.
Chamberlain features prominently in this authorised biography with almost two full column entries in the index.

211. Howard, C.H.D. "Joseph Chamberlain and the 'Unauthorized Programme' ", *English Historical Review* 65 (1950), 477–491.
An appreciative but critical review of J.L.Garvin's *Life of Joseph Chamberlain* volumes 1–3, concentrating in particular on flaws in the account of the unauthorised programme and its part in the 1885 election.

212. James, Robert Rhodes. "Radical Joe", *History Today* 7 (1957), 618–626.
This article traces Chamberlain's career in Liberal politics from 1873 until his break with Gladstone in 1886. It discusses the different ideologies of the two men, leading to Chamberlain's abandonment of Gladstone and Liberalism.

213. Jenkins, T.A. *Gladstone, Whiggery and the Liberal Party, 1874–1886* Oxford, 1988.

An analysis of the Whiggery prevalent at the commanding heights of the party against which Chamberlain struggled in vain. Argues that Chamberlain sought to establish a broad-based radicalism transcending sectional issues.

214. Simon, Alan. "Church Disestablishment as a Factor in the General Election of 1885", *Historical Journal* 18 (1975) 4, 791–820.
This article maintains that, thanks to Chamberlain, and much to Gladtone's embarrassment, the dominant issue at the 1885 election was disestablishment. Only Home Rule, even more controversial, displaced disestablishment from its high place on the political agenda.

215. Simon, Alan. "Joseph Chamberlain and Free Education in the Election of 1885", *History of Education* 2 (1973), 56–78.
Simon analyses the role of Chamberlain in directing, on the basis of his links with organised nonconformity, the campaign which led the Liberals to abandon their old tenderness for the voluntary sector of education.

216. Simon, Alan. "Joseph Chamberlain and the Unauthorised Programme". Oxford University D.Phil. dissertation, 1971.
This thesis examines the development of the unauthorised programme in the contest of Liberal Party politics. It maintains that Chamberlain was forced to articulate a more moderate manifesto than he had intended, and that ultimately he was left advocating a political radicalism which was out of date in the latter half of the 1880s.

ii. Chamberlain's Work as President of the Board of Trade, 1880–1885

217. Alderman, Geoffrey. "Joseph Chamberlain's Attempted Reform of the British Mercantile Marine", *Journal of Transport History* 1 (1972), 169–184.
An analysis of Chamberlain's efforts to promote merchant marine reform. The article traces the connections between

Chamberlain and Samuel Plimsoll and appraises both the depth of Chamberlain's commitment to reform and his success in achieving it when in government during the 1880s.

218. Jenkins, Roy. *Sir Charles Dilke: A Victorial Tragedy* London, 1958.
An elegant biography which devotes considerable space to Dilke's relationship with Chamberlain; the evidence for Chamberlain's complicity in Dilke's disgrace is weighed carefully with special attention to Mrs Crawford's visit to his house only two days before her confession in 1885.

219. Mallalieu, W.C. "Joseph Chamberlain and Workmen's Compensation", *Journal of Economic History* 10 (1950), 45–57.
Scholarly account of Chamberlain's efforts to secure compensation for working men who were victims of accidents at work.

iii. Chamberlain's Work as President of the Local Government Board, 1886

220. Dunbabin, J.P.D. "The Politics of the Establishment of County Councils", *Historical Journal* 6, no. 2 (1963), 226–252.
An account of the attempts, between 1870 and 1888, to establish elected county councils. The roles of Dodson, Joseph Chamberlain and Randolph Churchill are stressed.

C. CHAMBERLAIN AND THE IRISH QUESTION, 1881–1886

221. Goodlad, G.D. "Liberals and the Home Rule Issue, November 1885–July 1886: The Leaders and the Rank and File, with Special Reference to Certain Localities". Cambridge University Ph.D. dissertation, 1988.
An examination of how the Liberal Party, at constituency and at parliamentary level, came to embrace Home Rule. The dissenting role of Chamberlain and his base in Birmingham features significantly.

222. Griffiths, P.C. "The Caucus and the Liberal Party in 1886", *History* 61 (1976), 183–197.
Discusses how Chamberlain was unable to prevent local caucuses in the Liberal Party, with the major exception of Birmingham, from backing Gladstone's Home Rule policy.

223. Hamer, D.A. *John Morley: Liberal Intellectual in Politics* Oxford, 1958.
Interesting political biography and intellectual study which argues that Chamberlain's radicalism, based on the development of programmes, was diverging from Morley's, founded on the single issue, by the mid 1880s, and that this breach became obvious and beyond repair when the two men fell out over home rule.

224. Harrison, Henry. *Parnell, Joseph Chamberlain and Mr Garvin* London, 1938.
Refutes Garvin's version of the Parnell divorce intrigue as recounted in the official biography. Repeats and elaborates the accusations against Chamberlain made in *Parnell Vindicated.*

225. Harrison, Henry. *Parnell Vindicated: The Lifting of the Veil* London, 1931.
Harrison attempts to rescue Parnell's reputation, largely at the expense of Chamberlain who is portrayed as Captain O'Shea's political patron after 1882 and instrumental in Parnell's disgrace.

226. Howard, C.H.D. "Joseph Chamberlain, Parnell, and the Irish 'Central Board' Scheme, 1884–1885", *Irish Historical Studies* 8 (1952–1993), 324–361.
A detailed account of Chamberlain's flirtation with Parnell and his Irish party and of his attempt to settle the Irish question by proposing measures of self-government which stopped short of home rule.

227. Howard, C.H.D. "Joseph Chamberlain, W.H. O'Shea and Parnell, 1884, 1891–2", *Irish Historical Studies* 13 (1962), 33–38.

Relations between Chamberlain and Parnell, as shown by six letters in the Chamberlain papers at the University of Birmingham.

228. Howard, C.H.D. " 'The Man on a Tricycle': W.H. Duignan and Ireland 1881–1885", *Irish Historical Studies* 14 (1965), 246–260.
Six letters to Chamberlain from W.H. Duignan, an English supporter of Home Rule. Duignan's observations concern political feeling, views about coercion and local matters.

229. Loughlin, J.P. "Gladstone, Irish Nationalism and the Home Rule Question, 1882–1893, with Particular Reference to the Ulster problem". Trinity College, Dublin, Ph.D. dissertation, 1984.
Mainly about Gladstone's objectives in supporting Irish Home Rule, but there is interesting and serious analysis of the strengths of the Unionist case.

230. Lubenow, W.C. "Irish Home Rule and the Great Separation in the Liberal Party in 1886: The Dimensions of Parliamentary Liberalism". *Victorian Studies* 26 (1983), 162–180.
Lubenow argues that, Irish Home Rule aside, basic policy divisions between Liberal Unionists and Gladstonians were small and that radicals and radicalism in the Liberal Party both survived Chamberlain's departure.

231. Lubenow, W.C. *Parliamentary Politics and the Home Rule Crisis: The British House of Commons in 1886* Oxford, 1988.
An analysis of the crisis which determined the future course of Chamberlain's political life, set firmly in the context of a study of late nineteenth century parliamentary culture.

232. Lucy, H.W. "Mr Chamberlain and Home Rule", in Milner, A., et al., *Life of Joseph Chamberlain* London, 1914, 119–142.
A narrative account of the Home Rule crisis of 1885–1886 indicating Gladstone's responsibility for breaking up the party.

233. O'Day, Alan. *Parnell and the First Home Rule Episode 1884–1887* London, 1986.
An immensely detailed account of the home rule crisis, mainly from the perspective of the Parnellites but which devotes considerable space to analysis of Chamberlain's private role in these events.

234. Powell, J. Enoch. "Kilmainham—The Treaty that Never Was", *Historical Journal* 21 (1978), 913–937.
A re-examination of a letter, known as the "Kilmainham Treaty", written by Charles Stuart Parnell to William Henry O'Shea. Parnell is shown to be the victim of dirty tricks practised by O'Shea to which Chamberlain was, in part at least, privy.

235. Ryan, M.A. "The Home Rule Party and the British Empire". University of Dublin, M.A. dissertation, 1973.
There is no abstract available for this thesis, which could not be located in the library.

D. OUT OF OFFICE, 1886–1895

i. Chamberlain and Ireland, 1886–1895

236. Davies, Peter. "The Liberal Unionist Party and the Irish Policy of Lord Salisbury's Government, 1886–1892", *Historical Journal* 18 (1975), 85–104.
Argues that the Liberal Unionists led by Chamberlain were more concerned to maintain the government's stand against home rule than sponsor schemes for the "better administration of Ireland".

237. Loughlin, James. "Joseph Chamberlain, English Nationalism and the Ulster Question", *History* vol. 77, no. 250 (June 1992), 202–219.
Chamberlain's sympathetic view of prostestant Ulster is analysed in the context of his opposition to Gladstonian home rule. In terms of religion and race, it is argued, Ulster could

be integrated into Chamberlain's expanding concept of British nationalism.

238. Shannon, Catherine B. "The Ulster Liberal Unionists and Local Government Reform, 1885-98", *Irish Historical Studies* 18 (1973), 407–23.
Shows how Balfour, urged on by Ulster Liberal Unionists and by Chamberlain, adopted the Liberal Unionist alternative to home rule for Ireland. This alternative involved the introduction of a democratic system of local government and the encouragement of economic development.

ii. Chamberlain and Liberal Unionism, 1886–1895

239. Alcroft, D.H. "Joseph Chamberlain and the Politics of Central Birmingham 1889–1895". Birmingham University, M.A. dissertation, 1978.
A study of how Chamberlain used Birmingham as a personal political base, transforming it from a centre of radical Liberalism to the national capital of Unionism.

240. Davies, Peter. "The Role of the Liberal Unionist Party in British Politics, 1886–1895". London University (London School of Economics), Ph.D. dissertation, 1974.
A study of the origins of Liberal Unionism in the Home Rule crisis of 1886. It maintains that under Chamberlain's influence Liberal Unionism became a distinctive philosophy which helped to shape the programme upon which the Coalition government formed in June 1895 was based.

241. France, J.M. "Personalities and Politics in the Formation of the Unionist Alliance, 1885–1895". Cambridge University, Ph.D. dissertation, 1987.
A study in high politics which analyses the interaction of Chamberlain with, particularly, Salisbury, Balfour, Churchill and Hartington, and how they all contributed to the Unionist alliance.

242. Fraser, Peter. "The Liberal Unionist Alliance: Chamberlain, Hartington and the Conservatives 1886–1904". *English Historical Review* 77 (1962), 53–78.
Chamberlain's uneasy relationship with Hartington is analysed. The origins of their ultimate separation in 1904 are located in the problem of reconciling Chamberlain's democratic instinct with Hartington's more paternalistic outlook.

243. Goodman, Gordon L. "Liberal Unionism: The Revolt of the Whigs", *Victorian Studies* 3 (1959), 172–189.
Argues that the 1886 Liberal schism reflected a division between Whiggish conservative, wealthy interest and an increasingly radical democracy which supported Gladstone. The result was that Chamberlain found himself unable to create Liberal Unionism in a radical mould.

244. Hurst, M.C. *Joseph Chamberlain and Liberal Reunion. The Round Table Conference of 1887* London, 1967; Newton Abbot, 1970.
A classic account of the high politics of Liberal schism and the failure of "men of goodwill" to achieve reconciliation.

245. Hurst, M.C. "Joseph Chamberlain, the Conservatives and the Succession to John Bright, 1886–89". *Historical Journal* 7 (1964), 64–93.
A dense analysis of Chamberlain's role during the political party battles of the late 1880s. Chamberlain, like Bright, is portrayed as a 'National party' man committed to social reform whether implemented by Liberals or Conservatives.

246. Marsh, Peter T. *The Discipline of Popular Government: Lord Salisbury's Domestic Statecraft 1881–1902* Hassocks, 1978.
A penetrating study of Conservative politics centered on the subtle processes employed by Salisbury to reconcile his right wing with the more radical Chamberlainite Liberal Unionists after 1886.

E. CHAMBERLAIN IN THE UNITED STATES, 1887–1888

247. Maycock, Sir Willoughby. *With Mr Chamberlain in the United States and Canada, 1887–88* London, 1914.
An intimate and detailed account of Chamberlain's special mission to resolve the Canadian fisheries dispute. Maycock served as assistant secretary.

F. CHAMBERLAIN AND OLD AGE PENSIONS

248. Loch, C.S. *Old Age Pensions and Pauperism. An Inquiry into the Bearing of the Statistics on Pauperism Quoted by the Rt. Hon. J. Chamberlain, M.P., and Others, in Support of a Scheme for National Pensions* London, 1892.
Responding to Chamberlain's Birmingham speech, 21 April 1891, Loch argues that statistical evidence does not support the case for pensions.

G. COLONIAL SECRETARY, 1895–1903

i. Imperial Strategist and Administrator

249. Francis, Richard M. "The British Withdrawal from the Baghdad Railway Project in April 1903", *Historical Journal* 16, no. 1 (1973), 168–178.
Discusses how Chamberlain orchestrated opposition to British participation in the scheme—finally persuading Balfour to authorise withdrawal.

250. Friedberg, Aaron L. *The Weary Titan: Britain and the Experience of Relative Decline, 1895–1905* Princeton, 1988.
A stimulating study of how the British ruling elite responded to the erosion of strategic power and influence, in which Chamberlain's protectionist programme is mistakenly identified with support for an imperial *zollverein*.

251. Grenville, J.A.S. *Lord Salisbury and Foreign Policy: The Close of the Nineteenth Century* London, 1964.
A scholarly study in which Salisbury's preference for 'splendid isolation' is contrasted with Chamberlain's anxieties about the future security of the British Empire in the absence of an alliance with Germany and the United States.

252. Hardy, S.M. "Joseph Chamberlain and Some Problems of the 'Underdeveloped Estates' ". *University of Birmingham Historical Journal* 11 (1968), 170–190.
A critical assessment of Chamberlain's policy of aid for the underdeveloped countries in the British Empire, with special reference to the West Indies, West Africa and the foundation of the School of Tropical Medicine.

253. Humphreys, P.A. 'Anglo-American Rivalries and the Venezuela Crisis of 1895', *Transactions of the Royal Historical Society, 5th Series* 17 (1967), 131–164.
A discussion of the Venezuela crisis in the context of the relative power enjoyed by Britain and the United States in Latin America at the end of the nineteenth century. Chamberlain's attitudes to the dispute form a key part of the analysis.

254. Kennedy, Paul. *The Rise of the Anglo-German Antagonism, 1860–1914* London, 1980.
A magisterial study in which Chamberlain features as a key figure in Britain's abandonment of *laissez-faire* in favour of social imperialism.

255. Kubicek, Robert V. *The Administration of Imperialism: Joseph Chamberlain at the Colonial Office* Durham, N.C., 1969.
Scholarly treatment of Chamberlain's tenure arguing that constructive imperialism was checked by personal animosities and Treasury obstruction.

256. Kubicek, R.V. "Joseph Chamberlain and the Colonial Office: Study in Imperial Administration". Duke University, Ph.D. dissertation, 1965.

The argument is that administrative weakness inside the Colonial Office combined with Treasury parsimony to thwart Chamberlain's ambitions plans for colonial development.

257. Kubicek, Robert. "Joseph Chamberlain, the Treasury and Imperial Development 1895-1903", *Canadian Historical Association Annual Report* (1965), 105–116.
An account of the clash between Chamberlain's 'constructive imperialism' and desire for socio-economic improvements in the colonies financed by public expenditure, and the traditional penny-pinching views of the Treasury.

258. Monger, G.W. "The End of Isolation: Britain, Germany and Japan, 1900–1902", *Transactions of the Royal Historical Society* 13 (1963), 108–121.
Discusses the role of Chamberlain in trying to end Britain's isolation by advocating an alliance with Germany. In the end it was Lansdowne who ended isolation—but via an alliance with Japan.

259. Saul, S.B. "The Economic Significance of 'Constructive Imperialism' ", *Journal of Economic History* 17 (1957), 173–192.
Traces Chamberlain's conversion to "constructive imperialism" during his period as Colonial Secretary influenced by the Disraelian notion that protective tariffs in the Commonwealth and Empire would generate revenue for improvement schemes and strengthen ties to the Mother Country.

260. Warber, M.A. "The Imperial Policy of Joseph Chamberlain", Michigan State University, M.A. dissertation, 1990.
A study which uses Chamberlain's imperial policy as the foundation for exploring the validity of the theory of social imperialism.

261. Wilde, Richard H. "Joseph Chamberlain's Proposal of an Imperial Council in March, 1900", *Canadian Historical Review* 37 (1956), 225–246.
Argues that Chamberlain wanted to involve the self-govern-

ing colonies in an imperial council to reshape imperial defence once the Boer War finished, but was frustrated by opposition on the part of the Canadian government.

262. Williams, P.L. " 'The Rhetoric of Imperialism', the Speaking of Joseph Chamberlain 1895–1897", University of Missouri-Columbia, Ph.D. dissertation, 1972.
The thesis argues that Chamberlain's rhetoric, dwelling on the benefits of the colonies as sources of strength, pride and economic prosperity, was instrumental in the focusing of public attention on Imperial rather than domestic issues during the 1890s.

ii. Chamberlain and the Self-Governing Colonies

263. Burdon, R.M. *King Dick: A Biography of Richard John Seddon* Christchurch, N.Z., 1955.
Seddon, Prime Minister of New Zealand, loyally supported Chamberlain's efforts to promote empire unity at the Colonial Conferences of 1897 and 1902; he fell out with Chamberlain over New Zealand's claim to Fiji.

264. Crowlet, F.K. "A Vice-Regal Defendant: Sidelights on Westralian Federation", *Historical Studies. Australia and New Zealand* 9 (1960), 117–130.
Shows how Chamberlain removed the Governor of Western Australia from power after becoming scandalized by his financial speculations and indiscretions in the later 1890s. This crisis did not however prevent Western Australia from joining the new Commonwealth in 1900.

265. Deakin, Alfred, *The Federal Story: The Inner History of the Federal Cause* Melbourne, 1944.
Deakin, later Prime Minister of Australia, provides an excellent first-hand account in chapters XX-XXII of the "polite antagonism" which characterised negotiations between Chamberlain and the Australian delegation prior to Federation in 1900.

266. De Garis, B.K. "The Colonial Office and the Commonwealth Constitution Bill" in Martin, A.W. (ed.), *Essays in Australian Federation* Melbourne, 1969.
A critical view of Chamberlain's tactics as he sought amendments to the proposed Australian constitution between 1897 and 1900 using the Premier of New South Wales as an intermediary.

267. Ferguson, Bruce. *Rt. Hon. W.S. Fielding* Volume I, "The Mantle of Howe". Windsor, N.S., 1970; Volume II "Minister of Finance". Windsor, N.S., 1971.
The last chapter of volume I and the first chapter of volume II are concerned with the efforts of Fielding, Canada's Finance Minister, to secure from Chamberlain a positive response to Canadian trade preferences after 1897.

268. Garran, Sir Robert. "The Federation Movement and the Founding of the Commonwealth" in Scott, E. (ed.), *Cambridge History of the British Empire* Volume VIII, part I. Cambridge 1988.
Garran, in chapter XV, indicates the differences between Chamberlain and the Australian state premiers on the question of the Royal Prerogative in the 1900 Constitution.

269. La Nauze, J.A. *The Making of the Australian Constitution* Melbourne, 1944.
Chapter 16 provides an authoritative account of the negotiations between Chamberlain and the Australian delegation to London in 1900; La Nauze notes realistically that Chamberlain was distracted by South African affairs at the time.

270. Page, R.J.D. "Canada and the Empire during Joseph Chamberlain's Tenure as Colonial Secretary". Oxford University, D.Phil. dissertation, 1972.
A detailed study of Chamberlain's influence on Anglo- Canadian relations between 1895 and 1903 which covers the attempt to draw Canada into a closer relationship with the Empire.

271. Schull, Joseph. *Laurier: The First Canadian*, Toronto, 1965.
Laurier was Canada's Premier between 1896 and 1911. This biography is useful for its coverage of the stresses of Anglo-Canadian relations during Chamberlain's tenure at the Colonial Office.

272. Wilde, Richard H. "Joseph Chamberlain's Proposal of an Imperial Council in March 1900", *Canadian Historical Review* XXXVII (1956), 225–241.
A discussion of Chamberlain's proposed "Imperial Council", floated in a letter to Lord Minto in March 1900, and Laurier's lukewarm response.

iii. Chamberlain and South Africa

273. Anon. *An account of the Right Hon. Joseph Chamberlain's Visit to South Africa: A Record of Unique Practical Statesmanship* London, 1903.
A eulogistic narrative enlivened by a few photographs.

274. Anon. *Souvenir of Mr Chamberlain's South African Tour of 1902–1903* London, 1903.
Lavish, beautifully illustrated brochure produced by the *African Review* which includes a detailed itinery and reports of Chamberlain's major speeches.

275. Baylen, J.O. "W.T. Stead and the Boer War: The Irony of Idealism", *Canadian Historial Review* XL (1959), 304–314.
Baylen argues that Stead's animosity towards Chamberlain was focused by the Jameson Raid and the subsequent inquiry, leading Stead eventually into the pro-Boer camp.

276. Butler, Jeffrey. *The Liberal Party and the Jameson Raid* Oxford, 1968.
Interesting study of the Parliamentary impact of the Raid which argues that by the standards of political conduct then deemed acceptable, Chamberlain was not guilty of complicity.

277. Drus, Ethel. "The Chamberlain Papers Concerning Anglo-Transvaal Relations, 1896–1899", *Bulletin of the Institute of Historical Research* 27 (1954), 156–189.
Using Chamberlain's private papers this article attempts to show that Chamberlain contemplated war as the ultimate solution in the dispute between Britain and Transvaal after the Jameson Raid.

278. Drus, E. "The Question of Imperial Complicity in the Jameson Raid", *English Historical Review* 68 (1950), 582–594.
A detailed study of Chamberlain's part in the abortive Jameson Raid, and of the attempts to cover it up subsequently both in the House of Commons and in Garvin's *Life.*

279. Drus, E. "A Report on the Papers of Joseph Chamberlain Relating to the Jameson Raid and the Inquiry", *Bulletin of the Institute of Historical Research* 25 (1952), 33–62.
A dense analysis of the relevant documents which uses them to suggest that J.L. Garvin's account of the episode might be regarded as "special pleading".

280. Galbraith, John S. "The British South Africa Company and the Jameson Raid", *Journal of British Studies* 10, no. 1 (1970), 145–161.
Discusses the role of Chamberlain and Cecil Rhodes in the expansion of the British South Africa Company and argues that their irresponsibility contributed to the outbreak of the Boer War.

281. Gollin, A.M. *Proconsul in Politics. A Study of Lord Milner* London, 1964.
Chapter two covers Milner's role in South Africa from 1897 and argues that Chamberlain urged him to "work up to a crisis" in his relations with Kruger.

282. Griffiths, George. *With Chamberlain Through South Africa: A Narrative of the Great Trek* London, 1903.
"Joseph the Peacemaker" eulogised by the *Daily Mail*'s special correspondent in this account of his 1902–1903 tour.

283. Kesner, Richard M. "The Transvaal, the Orange River Colony and the South African Loan and War Contribution Act of 1903", *Albion* 10 (1978), 28–53.
Discusses the negotiation leading to the Act. Kesner argues that Chamberlain abandoned his demand for a large indemnity for the sake of long term political and economic objectives in South Africa.

284. Lockhart, J.G., and Woodhouse, C.M. *Rhodes* London, 1963.
Full biography which spends a lot of time trying to unravel the Jameson Raid and Chamberlain's part in it.

285. Longford, Elizabeth. *Jameson's Raid: The Prelude to the Boer War* London, 1960; new edition, 1982.
This study contains a well-written if ultimately conventional study of Chamberlain, and argues that although he was not complicit in the Jameson Raid he knew of the attempt to destabilize Transvaal in 1895.

286. Moore, Robert L. *Commission and Travels of H.M.S. Good Hope* Capetown, 1903.
A first hand account of Chamberlain's voyage to South Africa, 1902.

287. Porter, Andrew. "Lord Salisbury, Mr Chamberlain and South Africa 1895–1899", *Journal of Imperial and Commonwealth History* 1 (1972), 3–26.
This article suggests, contrary to the standard interpretations, that Salisbury did not oppose Chamberlain's South African policy because he agreed on the overriding importance of upholding British supremacy, which was under threat from the Boers.

288. Porter, A.N. *The Origins of the South African War: Joseph Chamberlain and the Diplomacy of Imperialism 1895–1899* Manchester, 1980.
Argues that Chamberlain as Colonial Secretary abandoned secret diplomacy in order to create an enlightened public opinion which would support the values and aims of Empire.

289. Roberts, Brian. *Cecil Rhodes: Flawed Colossus* London, 1987.
Chapter 13 includes an account of Rhodes' first meeting with Chamberlain; chapter 15 is useful on Chamberlain's relationship with Rhodes on the aftermath of the Jameson Raid.

290. Smith, Iain R. "The Origins of the South African War (1899–1902): A Re-Appraisal", *South African Historical Journal* 22 (1990), 24–60.
A scholarly review of recent historiography which places "the Chamberlain-Milner axis" in a wider framework of causes; especially informative on Chamberlain's attitude to the Uitlander franchise.

291. Wilde, R.H. "Joseph Chamberlain and South Africa", University of Wisconsin-Madison Ph.D. dissertation, 1951.
The University was unable to find this thesis in its collection.

292. Wilde, R.H. "Joseph Chamberlain and the South African Republic 1895–1899: A Study ion the Formulation of Imperial Policy", *Archives Year Book for South African History, Nineteenth Year I* Pretoria, 1957.
A study of imperial policy-making in the 1890s which focuses Chamberlain and his Colonial Office civil servants. "Day-to-day" considerations were more in evidence than "long-range" plans.

293. Wilson, Monica, and Thompson, Leonard. *The Oxford History of South Africa* Volume II, South Africa, 1870–1966. Oxford, 1971.
Thompson provides a penetrating assessment of Chamberlain's South African policy after 1895 arguing that he reversed the characteristic indecisiveness of the Colonial Office and pursued war to establish British supremacy in South Africa. Chamberlain and Milner were "the greatest recruiting agents" for Afrikaaner nationalism.

294. Winkler, Ralph. "Joseph Chamberlain and the Jameson Raid", *American Historical Review* 54 (1948–1949), 841–849.

Argues on the basis of evidence which he admits to be "inferential" that Chamberlain was complicit in the Jameson raid, 1895.

295. Woodhouse, C.M. "The Missing Telegrams and the Jameson Raid", *History Today* 12 (June 1962), 395–404. Woodhouse, C.M. "The Missing Telegrams and the Jameson Raid, Part 2", *History Today* 12 (July 1962), 506–514.
These two articles analyse the contents of telegrams, discovered at Rhodes House, Oxford, sent from London to Cape Town by officials of the British South Africa Company and associates of Cecil Rhodes, in the months prior to the Jameson Raid (1895). The conclusions drawn are that Chamberlain's complicity in the Raid has been much underestimated.

iv. Chamberlain and West Africa

296. Bryars, W.H. "Joseph Chamberlain and British Policy towards the Gold Coast and Ashanti Hinterland, 1895–1897". Birmingham University, M.Litt. dissertation, 1979.
A study of how Joseph Chamberlain tried to prevent French and German annexation of the Gold Coast hinterland, and of how he was partly frustrated by Salisbury's anxiety to avoid hinterland entanglement.

297. Dumett, R.E. "Joseph Chamberlain, Imperial Finance and Railway Policy in British West Africa in the Late Nineteenth Century", *English Historical Review* 90 (1975), 287–321.
Dumett, founding his case on West Africa, argues that Chamberlain's constructive imperialism involved battles with the Treasury, given that his schemes for colonial improvement conflicted with the ideal of the balanced budget and the nightwatchman state.

298. Oyemakinde, Wale. "Railway Construction and Operation in Nigeria, 1895–1911", *Journal of the History Society of Nigeria* 7 (1974), 302–324.
Discusses the socio-economic impact of railway construction in Nigeria and the positive role played by Chamberlain as

Colonial Secretary in encouraging railroad expansion in the colony.

v. Chamberlain and the West Indies

299. Will, H.A. "Colonial Policy and Economic Development in the British West India, 1895–1903", *Economic History Review* xxiii (1970), 129–147.
Will examines Chamberlain's determination to secure economic development in the West Indies and the bureaucratic and financial resistance he encountered on the part of local administrations, the British Treasury and the London capital market.

vi. Chamberlain and Denominational Schools

300. Ward, L.O. "Joseph Chamberlain and the Denominational Schools Question", *Journal of Educational Administration* 5 (1973), 21–24.
A short analysis of the reasons why Chamberlain was by 1896 prepared to defend church schools after having campaigned against them for over a quarter of a century.

vii. Chamberlain and Workmen's Compensation

301. Mallalieu, W.C. "Joseph Chamberlain and Workmen's Compensation", *Journal of Economic History*, 10 (1950), 45–57.
Scholarly account of the 1897 Workmen's (Compensation for Accidents) Act which sees it as a product of Chamberlain's attempts to push the Conservative Party into embracing social reforms.

H. CHAMBERLAIN AND TARIFF REFORM, 1903–1914

i. The Tariff Reform Campaign

302. Coetzee, Frans. *For Party or Country: Nationalism and the Dilemmas of Popular Conservatism in Edwardian England*

Oxford, 1990.
A valuable contribution to the literature on Edwardian Conservatism; chapter two sheds new light on the Chamberlainite Tariff Reform League.

303. Dark, Sidney. *The Life of Sir Arthur Pearson* London, 1922.
Chapters V and VI are especially useful for coverage of the tariff campaign between 1903 and 1905; Pearson threw his newspapers behind Chamberlain but their relationship was difficult.

304. Marrison, A.J. "Businessmen, Industries and Tariff Reform in Great Britain 1903–1930," *Business History* XXV (1983), 148–178.
Challenges the view that industrial attitudes towards tariff reform can be explained by reference to a clear-cut division between firms producing for the export market backing free trade and firms mostly reliant on the home market supporting protection.

305. Semmel, Bernard. *Imperialism and Social Reform: English Social-Imperial Thought 1895–1914* London, 1960.
This remains a stimulating study; tariff reform is firmly placed within the context of the ideology of social imperialism and the material interests of Chamberlain's supporters are usefully explored.

306. Summers, Anne. "The Character of Edwardian Nationalism, Three Popular Leagues", in Kennedy, P., and Nicholls, A. (eds.), *Nationalist and Racialist Movements in Britain and Germany before 1914* London, 1981, 66–87.
A useful account of Tariff Reform League activities set in the context of other movements, especially the Navy League and the National Service League.

307. Sykes, Alan. *Tariff Reform in British Politics, 1903–1913* Oxford, 1979.
A scholarly, comprehensive and insightful study of the high

politics of tariff reform drawing extensively on manuscript sources.

ii. Leader of the Tariff Reform Campaign, 1903–1906

308. Amery, L.S. "Mr Chamberlain and Fiscal Policy II", in Milner, A., et al. (eds.), *Life of Joseph Chamberlain* London 1914, 263–320.
Chamberlain's tariff campaign viewed as the climax of his career. Text is identical in places to Amery's later autobiography.

309. Amery, L.S. *My Political Life, vol. I, England Before the Storm 1896–1914* London, 1953.
The autobiography of a devoted acolyte, notable for its extravagant account of Chamberlain's Birmingham speech of May 1903, "as provocative as the theses which Luther nailed to the Church door at Wittenberg".

310. Cox, Harold. "Mr Chamberlain and Fiscal Policy I", in Milner, A., et al. (eds.), *Life of Joseph Chamberlain* London, 1914, 233–262.
An eminent free trader traces Chamberlain's *volte face* to his fears of imperial disintegration and his subsequent descent into protectionism.

311. McGoun, Archibald. *A Revenue Tariff within the Empire. Canadian Chapters on Mr Chamberlain's Policy* Montreal, 1904.
A sympathetic review of Chamberlain's tariff policy by a writer who articulates the idea that Canada's role is to serve as the granary of industrial Britain.

312. Marrison, A.J. "The Development of a Tariff Reform Policy during Joseph Chamberlain's First Campaign, May 1903–February 1904", in Chaloner, W.H., and Ratcliffe, Barrie M. (eds.), *Trade and Transport: Essays in Economic History in Honour of T.S. Willan* Manchester, 1977, 214–241.
A useful essay tracing the way in which Chamberlain's ideas

were moulded during the course of the debate which he initiated in May 1903.

313. Newton, Scott, and Porter, Dilwyn. *Modernization Frustrated: The Politics of Industrial Decline in Britain since 1900* London, 1988.
Chapter One places Chamberlain's tariff reform movement in the context of other marginalized modernization campaigns of the early twentieth century.

314. Porter, Dilwyn. "Joseph Chamberlain and the Origins of the Tariff Reform Movement", *Moirae: Journal of the School of Politics, Philosophy and History, Ulster Polytechnic* 3 (1978), 1–9.
Assesses the impact of Chamberlain's declaration for tariffs in the context of the developing movements for protection and constructive imperialism.

315. Porter, Dilwyn. "A Newspaper Owner in Politics. C. Arthur Pearson and the Tariff Reform League", *Moirae: Journal of the School of Politics, Philosophy and History, Ulster Polytechnic* 5 (1981), 111–121.
A study of Chamberlain's problematic relationship with Pearson, "the great hustler" and owner of the *Daily Express*.

316. Read, Donald. *Edwardian England 1901–15, Society and Politics* London, 1972.
This survey contains a useful chapter, "The Attack on Free Trade"; Chamberlain, Read argues, could not overcome "popular incomprehension" of his tariff policy.

317. Tomlinson, J. *Problems of British Economic Policy, 1870–1945* London, 1981.
Chapter 3 analyses the economic policy aspects of tariff reform, arguing that Chamberlain and his supporters conceptualized the economy in a way that was fundamentally different from orthodox free traders.

318. Zebel, Sydney. "Joseph Chamberlain and the Genesis of Tariff Reform", *Journal of British Studies* 7 (1967), 131–157.

Zebel indicates that Chamberlain was skeptical about free trader even in 1880; he was concerned throughout his career with both domestic reform and imperial consolidation. These twin concerns naturally led to the espousal of imperial preference.

iii. Chamberlain and Tariff Reform: Illness and Semi-Retirement, 1906–1914

319. Dutton, David. "Life beyond the Political Grave: Joseph Chamberlain 1906–14", *History Today* 34 (1984), 23–28.
Discusses the influence of Joseph Chamberlain on the Unionist Party in the years after his stroke in 1906. The author argues that the illness was a setback to Chamberlain's project of transforming the Unionist Party into a party of constructive social reformers.

iv. The Tariff Commission

320. Marrison, A.J. "British Businessmen and the 'Scientific' Tariff: A Study of Joseph Chamberlain's Tariff Commission, 1903–21". University of Hull, Ph.D. dissertation, 1980.
This thesis examines the ideology behind, and the membership of, the Tariff Commission, before embarking on an explanation of its enquiries into sectors of the economy. It argues that the work of the Commission, far from being 'scientific', became increasingly propagandist.

321. Marrison, A.J. "The Tariff Commission, Agricultural Protection and Food Taxes, 1903–13", *Agricultural History Review* 34 (1986), 171–187.
This article traces the rise and fall of agricultural protection as an item in the manifesto of the tariff reform campaign.

v. Tariff Reform and Party Politics, 1903–1914

322. Blewitt, Neal. "Free Fooders, Balfourites, Whole Hoggers. Factionalism within the Unionist Party, 1906–10.", *Historical*

Journal 11 (1968), 95–124.
An analysis of how the tariff reformers ("whole hoggers") captured control of the Unionist Party between 1906–1910, via the conversion of Balfour (1909) and the penetration of constituency organisations.

323. Cain, Peter. "Political Economy in Edwardian England: The Tariff Reform Controversy", in O'Day, Alan (ed.), *The Edwardian Age: Conflict and Stability* London, 1979, 35–59.
An analysis of the economic thinking which underpinned Chamberlain's last crusade set in the context of party political strife in the Edwardian period.

324. Dutton, David. "Unionist Politicians and the Aftermath of the General Election of 1906. A Reassessment", *Historical Journal* 22 (1979), 861–876.
Dutton argues that the Chamberlainites prevailed over Balfour in the struggle over party organisation and ideology which followed the 1906 election defeat.

325. Fraser, Peter. "Unionism and Tariff Reform and the Crisis of 1906", *Historical Journal* 5 (1962), 149–166.
Discusses the Chamberlain-Balfour controversy of 1906 in the context of a power struggle for control of Conservative policy between the constituency associations and the parliamentary leadership.

326. Gollin, A.M. *Balfour's Burden: Arthur Balfour and Imperial Preference* London, 1935.
A well-documented study detailing Balfour's efforts to keep his government together after Chamberlain had opened a rift on the tariff issue in 1903.

327. Green, E.H.H. "Radical Conservatism in Britain, 1899–1903". University of Cambridge, Ph.D. dissertation, 1986.
This study identifies radical conservatism with support for tariff reform and national-imperial economic autarky. It focuses on those within the Conservative Party who argued for the protectionist strategy and discusses their failure.

328. Green, E.H.H. "Radical Conservatism: The Electoral Genesis of Tariff Reform", *Historical Journal* 28 (1985), 667–692.
Discusses how Chamberlain's programme of popular imperialism and tariff-financed social reform provided the Conservative party with an electoral strategy which would court the new working class vote.

329. Holland, Bernard. *The Life of Spencer Compton, Eighth Duke of Devonshire* London, 1911.
Chapter XXVII of this two volume, official biography provides a well-documented narrative of the Duke's deteriorating relationship with Chamberlain during the tariff controversy.

330. Judd, Denis. *Balfour and the British Empire: A Study in Imperial Evolution, 1874–1932* London, 1968.
A perceptive study of Balfour which contains a full account of the cabinet and party crisis provoked by Chamberlain's tariff reform crusade after 1903.

331. MacKay, Ruddock F. *Balfour, Intellectual Statesman* Oxford, 1985.
Balfour's object—"to provide firm, economical and effective government"—is thwarted when Chamberlain "rocks the boat" in chapter eight of this biography.

332. Porter, D. "The Unionist Tariff Reformers 1903–1914", University of Manchester, Ph.D. dissertation, 1976.
This thesis discusses the ideology and composition of the Tariff Reform League, and the effects of its campaign on the Unionist Party. It concludes that the Unionist abandonment of food taxes in 1913 had a shattering impact on the tariff reform movement.

333. Rempel, Richard A. *Unionists Divided. Arthur Balfour, Joseph Chamberlain and the Unionist Free Traders* Newton Abbot, 1972; Hamden, Conn., 1972.
A useful study drawing on manuscript sources which charts the course of intra-party strife unleashed by Chamberlain's tariff policy.

334. Russell, A.K. *Liberal Landslide. The General Election of 1906* Newton Abbot, 1973; Hamden, Conn., 1973.
Valuable in its analysis of tariff reform as an election issue; Russell concludes that Chamberlain committed crucial tactical errors.

335. Scally, Robert J. *The Origins of the Lloyd George Coalition. The Politics of Social-Imperialism, 1900–1918* Princeton, N.J., 1975.
A penetrating study of British social-imperialism which sets tariff reform firmly in an appropriate ideological context.

336. Turner, B.H.P. "Tariff Reform and the Conservative Party, 1895–1906". London University (London School of Economics) Ph.D. dissertation, 1966.
Barely adequate account of the origins of the tariff reform movement drawing on a surprisingly limited range of sources.

I. CHAMBERLAIN'S POLITICAL PHILOSOPHY

337. Fraser, Derek. "Joseph Chamberlain and the Municipal Ideal", *History Today* 37 (1987), 33–39.
Fraser examines Chamberlain's "municipal socialism", locating its origins in the commitment to civic service and in concern to improve educational provision within Birmingham.

338. Grainger, J.H. *Patriotisms: Britain 1900–1939* London, 1986.
Chapters 11 and 12 locate Chamberlain amongst other "imperial statesmen" and assess tariff reform as one of a range of "patriotic persuasions".

339. Hall, E.P., Jr. "Localism in Joseph Chamberlain's Social Politics, 1869–1895", University of Massachusetts, Ph.D. dissertation, 1977.
The thesis examines Chamberlain's commitment to 'localism', based on community organisation around local govern-

ment rather than the state. It concludes that Chamberlain was really concerned with wider issues of national power.

340. Hurst, Michael. "Joseph Chamberlain and Late-Victorian Liberalism", Durham University Journal 66 (1973), 60–75.
Chamberlain's relationship with the Liberal Party up to 1892 is traced. It is argued that by 1888 Chamberlain was no longer a Liberal in the strictest sense of the term, while without his influence Gladstonian Liberalism languished.

341. Mock, Wolfgang. "The Function of Race on Imperialist Ideologies: The Example of Joseph Chamberlain", in Kennedy, P., and Nicholls, A. (eds.), *Nationalist and Racialist Movements in Britain and Germany before 1914* London, 1981, 190–201.
A brief but useful analysis of Chamberlain's ideas about race. He is described as a "mainstream racialist" reflecting the ideas of external social Darwinism.

342. Powell, J. Enoch. "The Myth of Empire ce n'est que l'Illusion qui Dure?" *Round Table* 240 (1970), 435–444.
Argues that imperial statesmen, including Chamberlain and Milner, clung to programmes which had little chance of being realised, but that this self-deception may be a national survival mechanism.

343. Quinault, Roland. "John Bright and Joseph Chamberlain", *Historical Journal* 28 (1985), 623–646.
This article points out the ideological similarity of Bright to Chamberlain by examining the attitudes of both to a range of issues, such as education, land reform, franchise extension and home rule. It concludes that Bright was a more successful reformer.

J. JOSEPH CHAMBERLAIN'S LEGACY IN BIRMINGHAM

344. Briggs, Asa. *History of Birmingham* Volume II, Borough and City, 1865–1938. Oxford, 1952.
Chapter IV provides a succinct, authoritative account of how

Birmingham became "the best-governed city" with due recognition of Chamberlain's civic vision.

345. Cannadine, David. "The Calthorpe Family and Birmingham, 1810–1910: A 'Conservative Interest' Examined", *Historical Journal* 28 (1975), 725–760.
A study of the influence wielded in Birmingham politics by the Calthorpe family and how this was undermined by the mobilisation of the middle class as a result of parliamentary reform and the campaigning politics of Joseph Chamberlain.

346. Fraser, Derek. *Power and Authority in the Victorian City* Oxford, 1979.
Chapter Four locates Chamberlain's municipal reforms in the broad context of the development of local government in mid nineteenth century Birmingham.

347. Hurst, M.C. *Joseph Chamberlain and West Midland Politics 1886–1895* Oxford, 1962.
A dense, 'high politics' analysis of Chamberlain's use of his political base in Birmingham to create an alliance between Liberal Unionism and Tory Democracy. At times so detailed that wider conclusions become rather obscure.

348. Thomson, A.P.D. "The Chamberlain Memorial Tower, University of Birmingham", *University of Birmingham Historical Journal* 4 (1954), 167–179.
A scholarly account of Chamberlain's part in the construction of the famous tower or campanile at Birmingham University. It was felt, with justification, that the landmark would become a local talking-point and attract students to the new University.

349. Whates, H.R.G. *The Birmingham Post, 1857–1957* Birmingham, 1957.
An informative centenary volume which casts useful light on Chamberlain's relationship with the *Post*; especially valuable for home rule and tariff reform.

Chapter Seven

Personal and Professional Life

350. Anon. "Indication of Houses of Historical Interest in London" Part XLIV. 1915.
This pamphlet is partly devoted to 26 Highbury Place, the house where Joseph Chamberlain lived from the age of nine until his departure for Birmingham.

351. Chamberlain, Sir Austen. *Down the Years* London, 1935.
Essays recalling, amongst others, Balfour and Morley, and reflecting on their relationships with Austens' father.

352. Chamberlain, J. Austen. *Notes on the Families of Chamberlain and Harben* privately printed, 1915.
Austen's research relating to his grandparents and their ancestors.

353. Chamberlain, Sir Austen. *Politics from Inside: An Epistolary Chronicle, 1906–1914* London, 1936.
Mainly Austen's letters, "above all for my father", written during Chamberlain's protracted last illness.

354. Dilkes, David. *Neville Chamberlain* Volume I, Pioneering and Reform, 1869–1929, Cambridge, 1984.

Chapters one and two locate Neville in the context of family life and are enlightening on the relationship with his father whose influence, it is suggested, he never escaped.

355. Dutton, David. *Austen Chamberlain: Gentleman in Politics* Bolton, 1985.
Dutton argues that Joseph tried to make his son into a politician; Austen, however, did not possess his father's radical political enthusiasm.

356. Feiling, Keith. *The Life of Neville Chamberlain* London, 1946.
Chapters I to VIII contain a narrative account of Neville's childhood, youth and early manhood, with references to his father.

357. Laing, Diane Whitehill. *Mistress of Herself* Barre, Mass., 1965.
A well-written, intimate biography of "Cousin Mary", i.e. Mary Endicott, Chamberlain's third wife.

358. Morley, John. *Recollections* 2 vols. London, 1917.
Morley's first volume is invaluable for his memories of his personal and political friendship with Chamberlain between 1873 and 1886.

359. Pownall, David. *My Father's House*, 1991.
Play, first performed by Birmingham Repertory Theatre on 28 October 1991, focusing on Joseph Chamberlains's relationship with his children, especially Neville. Programme by Proscenium Advertising, Bristol, contains useful background articles on the Chamberlain dynasty and on "the best governed city in the world".

360. Seymour-Jones, C. *Beatrice Webb: Woman of Conflict* London, 1992.
Chapter IX, "Radical Joe", details the unhappy course of Beatrice's love affair with Chamberlain; in her view he required "intelligent servility" in a wife.

361. Smith, Barbara M.D. "Chamberlain, Arthur (1842–1913), Metal Goods and Ammunition Manufacturer", in Jeremy, David J. (ed.), *Dictionary of Business Biography* Volume I. London, 1984, 633–643.
A well-researched and informative article detailing the successful business career of Joseph's younger brother.

Chapter Eight

Historiographical Materials

A. GENERAL PLACE IN HISTORY, INFLUENCE, ETC.

362. Anon. "The Decline and Fall of Joseph Chamberlain: The Great Imperialist Turns Parochial", *Times Literary Supplement* (17 August 1969), 869–870.
A review of Julian Amery's *Life of Joseph Chamberlain, Volume V, 1901–1903* and Volume VI, 1903–1968.

363. Balfour, Michael. *Britain and Joseph Chamberlain* London, 1985.
Magisterial volume which evaluates Chamberlain's career in the context of the problems and opportunities confronting a mature industrial society and world power.

364. Brown, Harry. *Joseph Chamberlain, Radical and Imperialist* London, 1974.
A thin potted biography of Chamberlain with a useful set of documents and bibliographical references.

365. Clarke, Peter. "Marching with the Majority", *Times Literary Supplement* (1 May 1981), 493.

A review of Richard Jay's *Joseph Chamberlain: A Political Study* which traces the highlights of his career in politics.

366. Clarke, Peter. "The Steamroller from Birmingham", *Times Literary Supplement* (13 May 1977), 586.
A review of Judd's *Radical Joe* which argues that Chamberlain's radicalism was, over the last twenty years of his life, that of the right wing populist.

367. Gollin, Alfred. "Historians and the Great Crisis of 1903", *Albion* 8, no. 1 (1976), 83–97.
A historiographical essay which argues that British setbacks in the Boer War led Chamberlain to prove that Britain could govern its distant colonies.

368. Gulley, Elsie Elizabeth. "Joseph Chamberlain and English Social Politics". Columbia University Ph.D. dissertation, 1926.
A pioneering study of Chamberlain's impact on social policy and politics in the late nineteenth century. It argues that the "New Liberals" adopted Chamberlainite social policies after 1906. Thus "Radical Joe" triumphed vicariously.

369. Gulley, Elsie Elizabeth. *Joseph Chamberlain and English Social Politics* New York, 1926.
Published version of entry #368.

370. Hughenden Foundation. *The Imperial Idea and the European Idea* London, 1986.
Two pamphlets containing essays by Julian Amery, Joseph Egerton and David Nicholson which trace the links between Chamberlain's philosophy of constructive reform, imperial co-operation, and protection, and the contemporary European idea.

371. James, Robert Rhodes. "Prince of Opportunists?" *Spectator* 28 October 1966, 561.
Review of Peter Fraser's *Joseph Chamberlain* and of D.H.

Elletson's *The Chamberlains* containing some standard observations.

372. Johnson, Paul. "The Man Who Smashed Parties", *New Statesman* (8 August 1969), 183–184.
Review of Volumes V and VI of Julian Amery's biography. Johnson makes some conventional comments about Chamberlain and the impact of tariff reform on the Conservative government of Arthur Balfour.

373. Koss, Stephen. *The Rise and Fall of the Political Press in Britain, Volume I: The Nineteenth Century* London, 1981; *Volume II: The Twentieth Century* London, 1984.
Chamberlain features frequently in this authoritative account of the relations between the press and the politicians. He is revealed in volume one as manipulative and inclined to leak. The first chapter of volume two deals with the press during the tariff campaign.

374. MacDonald, J. Ramsay. "Mr Chamberlain as a Social Reformer", in Milner, A., et al. (eds.), *Life of Joseph Chamberlain* London, 1914, 143–193.
A significant analysis placing Chamberlainite reforms in the context of the erosion of *laissez-faire.*

375. M.M. "Joseph Chamberlain—A Summary of His Career", in Milner, A., et al. (eds.) *Life of Joseph Chamberlain* London, 1914, 9–73.
A straightforward, narrative summary of Chamberlain's career.

376. Porter, Andrew. "Joseph Chamberlain: A Radical Reappraised", *Journal of Imperial and Commonwealth History* 6 (1978), 330–336.
A review of Judd's *Radical Joe* which argues that Chamberlain genuinely tried both to make his country a better place to live in and to protect its international interests. Judd is criticised for a rather superficial approach to some important issues in Chamberlain's public career.

377. Quinault, Roland. "Joseph Chamberlain: A Reassessment", in Gourvish, T.R., and O'Day, Alan (eds.), *Later Victorian Britain 1867–1900* London, 1988, 69–92.
An important, sceptical assessment which argues that Chamberlain's contribution to late Victorial politics has been exaggerated.

378. Skidelsky, Robert. "Radical Joe and Logical Enoch", *Spectator* (12 November 1977), 19–20.
A critical review of Enoch Powell's *Joseph Chamberlain.*

379. Spender, J.A. "Mr Chamberlain as a Radical", in Milner, A., et al. (eds.), *Life of Joseph Chamberlain*, London, 1914, 74–118.
A significant essay from the editor of the liberal *Westminster Gazette* indicating respect for Chamberlain's unauthorised programme.

380. Stephens, W.B. (ed.). *A History of the County of Warwick* volume VII, The City of Birmingham. London 1964.
This volume in the prestigious Victoria History of the Counties of England series contains numerous references to Chamberlain and his connection with Birmingham both in local and national politics.

381. Strauss, William L. *Joseph Chamberlain and the Theory of Imperialism* Washington, D.C., 1942.
Chamberlain's ideas set in the context of a rather undiscriminating review of contemporary ideas on empire and race.

B. BIBLIOGRAPHIES

382. Holli, Melvin G. "Joseph Chamberlain and the Jameson Raid. A Bibliographical Survey", *Journal of British Studies* 3 (1964), 152–166.
A historiographical study of the way in which Chamberlain's role in the Jameson Raid has been viewed.

383. Library of Congress. *Select List of References on the British Tariff Movement* Washington D.C., 1904; second edition, 1906.
An excellent guide to the contemporary literature of tariff

reform; the second edition includes an appendix listing works published between 1904 and 1906 compiled by A.P.C. Griffin, Chief Bibliographer.

384. Porter, Andrew. "In memoriam Joseph Chamberlain: A Review of Periodical Literature, 1960–73", *Journal of Imperial and Commonwealth History* 3 (1975), 295–297.
This article reviews periodical literature concerning Chamberlain in an effort to understand shifting historiographic and public views of the man from the 1880s until his death in 1914.

385. Royal Commission on Historical Manuscripts (based on the National Register of Archives). *Papers of British Cabinet Ministers 1782–1900* London, 1982.
A guide to the location of Cabinet Ministers Papers. Chamberlain is featured.

386. University of Birmingham. *Handlist to the Papers of Joseph Chamberlain: With Revisions up to February 1984* Birmingham, 1984).

387. Researchers wishing to pursue the major issues with which Chamberlain was concerned as a Cabinet minister will find Peter Cockton's five volume *Subject Catalogue of the House of Commons Parliamentary Papers 1801–1900*, published by Chadwyck-Healey, Cambridge, 1988, to be invaluable. This comprehensive listing may be usefully supplemented by reference to Hilda Vernon Jones' *Catalogue of Parliamentary Papers 1801–1900*, published by P.S. King & Son, Westminster, 1903, and the supplementary volume covering *Parliamentary Papers 1901–1910*, published in 1912. These earlier catalogues contain useful content summaries of major items. Chamberlain's tenure at the Board of Trade between 1880–1885 generated references in volume II of the Chadwyck-Healey *Catalogue*. The Bankruptcy Bill of 1883 has attracted little attention from historians to date so a source such as a Board *Memorandum* at 1883 (85) LV. 59 showing the effect of the proposed changes in the law is an appropriate starting point. There is also a useful *Report on Bankruptcy Bill Pro-*

ceedings attributed to the Standing Committee on Trade, Shipping and Manufactures at 1883 (224) XI. 235.

Proposals by Mr Chamberlain for Establishing Local Marine Courts, dating from October 1883, are located in the House of Commons Papers at 1884 (74) LXXI. 157. Further material which links directly to Chamberlain's thwarted Merchant Shipping Bill is the *Letter from the President of the Board of Trade to the Liverpool Steamship Owners Association* at 1884 (125) LXXI. 405; also his *Letter to Shipowners and Underwriters with Reference to the Merchant Shipping Bill* at 1884 (193) LXXI. 257.

The "Chamberlain Circular", a significant landmark in the history of unemployment relief policy dating from Chamberlain's brief tenancy at the Local Government Board is to be found amongst *Circular Letters by the Local Government Board to Boards of Guardians and Vestries and District Boards in the Metropolis with Reference to Pauperism and Distress* at 1886 (69) LVI. 179. His continuing interest in social policy was reflected by membership of the Royal Commission on the Aged Poor in 1895. The Commission's *Report* and *Minutes of Evidence* are in the House of Commons Papers at 1895 [Cd 7684 I, II] XIV, XV.

Volume V of the Chadwyck-Healey *Catalogue* lists papers concerned with the Dominions and the Colonies. At 1895 [Cd 7824] LXX. 199 are to be found various *Despatches from the Secretary of State for the Colonies on Questions of Trade and Commercial Treaties*; the Proceedings of Chamberlain's 1897 Colonial Conference are located at 1897 [Cf 8596] LIX. 631. These documents will interest any researcher concerned with Chamberlain's quest for imperial integration and the origins of his tariff reform policy.

South African affairs are prominently represented in House of Commons papers after 1895. These are listed on pp. 172–175 of the Chadwyck-Healey *Catalogue*. Chamberlain was most personally involved with the Select Committee on British South Africa which investigated his conduct in relation to the Jameson Raid. The Committee's proceedings are the subject of a *Report* at 1896

(380) IX. 47. Official correspondence with Cecil Rhodes concerning his proposed extension to the Bechuanaland Railway is to be found at 1899 [Cd 9323] LXIII. 215. House of Commons Papers relating to Colonial and particularly South African affairs in the last three years of Chamberlain's ministerial career are listed in *Parliamentary Papers 1901–1910*, especially pp. 67–70.

Chapter Nine

Iconography

A. HIGHBURY

Highbury was the home of Joseph Chamberlain from 1880 until 1914. After Joseph's death Highbury was used first as an annexe to the First Southern General Hospital and then as a home for disabled ex-servicemen. In 1919 Sir Austen Chamberlain gave the house to the Highbury Trustees who presented it to the Corporation of Birmingham in 1932. From then until 1984 it was used as a Home for Aged Women, although what had been the Library was simultaneously transformed into a museum.

In 1984 the aged women departed and the City Council embarked on an extensive renovation and restoration programme. It now serves three purposes: first, as a conference and banqueting centre; second, as a Museum; and third, as a historic house and garden which is open to the public on a set number of days (usually Sundays and Bank Holidays) each year.

Information about hospitality at Highbury is available from Birmingham City Council, Catering Service Unit, Highbury, 4 Yew Tree Road, Moseley, Birmingham, B13 8QG (tel. 021 449 6549, fax 021 442 4782). The Joseph Chamberlain Memorial Museum is cared for by the Social History Department of Birmingham Museum, with advice on the care and preservation of the house interior and furnishings being provided by the Department of Applied Art. The Department of Social History organises the open days for the general public and will arrange appointments with interested historians who wish for a personal guided tour.

Highbury was designed for Joseph Chamberlain by the Birmingham architect John Henry Chamberlain (no relation) and built by the Birmingham firm of John Barnsley and Sons. Features of the house are:

The Hall. This two-storey room occupies the whole central area of the house. It was designed so that entertaining could be easily organised. There is a central brass downlighter made by John Hardman and Company, Birmingham. After initially being fitted for gas lighing Highbury was converted to electricity in the mid 1880s; it may have been the first Birmingham private house to have been so equipped. The walls are decorated with elaborate marquetry panels, blue and white tiles with a design of passion flowers and gold and white plaster panels of horse-chesnuts and sunflowers. There are five oak wall-cabinets which were originally used to display oriental china and other ornaments presented to Joseph. There is a brass grille for the central heating system in a recess below the stairs. The system was installed at the time of the house's construction.

The Museum. This used to be the library. It has now been restored to its original appearance. The Library is not Joseph's: it has been recreated by donation. The rest of the room however comprises authentic 'Chamberlainiana' (with the exception of the desk, which is an exact copy of the one used by Joseph Chamberlain himself—the whereabouts of the original is now unknown). Items of interest include Joseph's pipe, tobacco and cigar boxes; his last orchid buttonhole; his cigar case as it was at the time of his death (with two cigars unsmoked) and a chair used by both Joseph and by Neville. There is a selection of photographs showing scenes of Birmingham life before and after the slum clearance programme, and a study of Joseph, unmonocled, in his days as a local politician. Finally, the museum contains a collection of miscellania associated with Chamberlain: a Joseph Chamberlain jack-in-the-box, Toby jug, tile and plate; a Tenniel pencil drawing of 1894 (" 'quousque tandem' or one at a time") illustrating disagreement between Arthur Balfour and Chamberlain about whether Liberal Unionists or Conservatives should contest forthcoming by-elections at Hythe and Leamington and a statuette with Chamberlain's injunction 'Learn to think imperially' engraved on the base.

Drawing Room. This was used for receiving visitors in the afternoons and for entertaining guests after dinner. On the ceiling there are painted motifs and inlaid panels of satinwood and walnut, while the doors and dado are of walnut with panels of sycamore. The room contains a portrait of Joseph's third wife (nee Mary Endicott), by Sir John Everett Millais. It was commissioned by Joseph shortly after the marriage in 1888 and finished in 1891.

Upstairs. There are stained glass windows with unusual animal and marine life designs. The wall is covered in anaglypta, an early example of this technique. On the landing there are portraits of Austen, Neville and of course Joseph himself. This last was completed in 1924 by Nestor Cambra, after the portrait by Hubert von Herkomer. It was presented on the opening of the new Unionist Headquarters in Birmingham. There is in addition an unsigned oil painting of Joseph in the master bedroom.

The Grounds. These are most extensive. Access is gained via the south-facing terrace. The house was built in a small suburb of Birmingham, Moor Green, just outside Moseley, which was at the time semi-rural but conveniently close to the railway station at King's Heath. The privacy of the estate was maintained as development encroached upon the surrounding countryside to the south, by large-scale planting of trees.

The layout was designed by a Surrey landscape architect, Edward Milner. The nearby fields were used as a small farm. The park contains a small lake (built from an existing stream) and a rock garden laid out in 1901 to Chamberlain's own design, as well as an 'Italian' garden. Eighteen gardeners were employed to maintain the gardens.

The Exterior of the House. Like the interior this is decorated with themes from the natural world—vines, strawberries, lilies, laurels and sunflowers adorn the terracotta mouldings and carved stone work.

During Joseph's lifetime a large complex of greenhouses adjoined the house. There were in fact thirteen, containing Chamberlain's justly famous orchid collection as well as a range of other exotic plants. Chamberlain's active interest in botanical life was frequently rewarded with prizes.

B. BIRMINGHAM MUSEUM OF SCIENCE AND INDUSTRY

Two boxes of photographs held by the Social History Department at the Birmingham Museum of Science and Industry are of interest though some prints in this collection duplicate material in the Heslop Room at Birmingham University Library. The boxes are labelled "King's Norton: Highbury".[1]

Box 1 contains about fifty prints, mainly interior and exterior studies of the Chamberlain family home taken by Dennis Assinder in 1986 and 1987. Some late nineteenth and early twentieth century prints are included. The earliest, dated May 1889, shows Mrs Chamberlain, Beatrice, Austen and others in the hall. There are several views of the gardens, the orchid houses and various exotic plants taken in 1892 by Cooper, an understandably proud head gardener. One print, dated October 1902, catches the Colonial Secretary off-duty in the rock garden.

The first section of Box 2 contains about twenty photographs of Chamberlain and various members of his family dating mostly from 1892. Joe is portrayed both with and without his famous monocle. Two snapshots capture Chamberlain in Ladysmith during his South African visit of 1902–1903. The second section of Box 2 contains recent black and white photographs of various artefacts to be found at Highbury. It is interesting to note that the Birmingham radical, sometimes labelled "the English Gambetta", kept a framed photograph of the founder of the Third Republic on the mantelpiece in his library. A third section contains photographs of Highbury in use as a military hospital.

C. BIRMINGHAM CENTRAL LIBRARY

Amongst the ephemera in the Birmingham Collection at the Central Library are two cartoon portraits by "Spy" (Leslie Ward) which originally appeared in *Vanity Fair*. The Birmingham Collection also contains a significant holding of postcards dealing humourously with various aspects of Chamberlain's politics in the years 1902–1906. Though these are listed under two separate headings (Accession numbers 373701 and 453600), they are now held in one box.

Researchers with a particular interest in the gardens at Highbury would find it useful to consult the catalogues of plants and orchids collected by Joseph Chamberlain. These were published in connection with the sale of Highbury by Messrs Protheroe and Morris in 1915 (Accession numbers 259564 and 259695). Two bronze medallions, struck by J.A. Restall of Birmingham, were removed from the Central Library in 1983 and are now held by the Birmingham City Museum and Art Gallery. One dates from c.1903 and commemorates the tariff reform campaign; the other celebrates Chamberlain's seventieth birthday in 1906.

D. THE CHAMBERLAIN MEMORIAL

The Chamberlain Memorial, located in Chamberlain Square, was erected in 1880 "in gratitude for public service given to this town". Its inscription records, in particular, the municipalisation of the gas and water supplies "to the great and lasting benefit of the inhabitants". The Memorial incorporates a medallion portrait executed in Sicilian marble by Thomas Woolner R.A.[2]

E. UNIVERSITY OF BIRMINGHAM LIBRARY, OLD FAMILY PHOTOGRAPHS

This collection of family photographs is located at C9/1–4 and C9/5–28 in the Chamberlain archive held in the Rare Books and Manuscripts Reading Room, University of Birmingham (see chapter 3). This collection contains a voluminous set of photographs relating to the Chamberlains.

As far as Joseph is concerned the collection may be divided into two separate categories: (a) old family photographs and (b) photographs relating to Joseph and Mary Chamberlain.

Category (a) is held within the miscellaneous collection of items relating to Joseph, Mary and Austen Chamberlain. It comprises loose photographs and a set of three albums. For the most part the subjects are Joseph, his wives, his in-laws and his children, usually photographed in formal style (though there are occasional snapshots). There is in addition the occasional shot of Highbury Hall and of close political colleagues such as Jesse Collings.

Category (b) is also held within the miscellaneous collection. It comprises a mixture of the private and the political. There are holiday photographs (people and landscapes), along with shots recording some of the great public occasions in Joseph's life. Examples are the 1902–1903 South African tour, campaigning in the 1906 General Election, and a study taken at the age of 70. There are, in addition, some rare and unusual items hidden among the photographs. Three which stand out are a Max Beerbohm cartoon of Joseph; a pencil sketch of Joseph's luggage at Edinburgh Station, October 1901; and an 1852 proclamation—no doubt kept by Joseph because of its relevance to the tariff reform debates. The proclamation was made on behalf "of the working classes of Great Britain", as represented by the Metropolitan Trades' Delegates. It inveighed against free trade and unrestricted competition and commended the cause of protection for domestic industry and workers, on the grounds that this would prevent exploitation and encourage prosperity and employment for all.

NOTES

1. See Darby Stafford, "The Colonial Secretary's Country House" (illustrated with photographs), *The English Illustrated Magazine* xxv (April–June 1901) (Birmingham Central Library Acc. No. 158234).

2. See B. Pugh, *Solid Citizens: Statues in Birmingham* Sutton Coldfield, 1983.

Chapter Ten

Pamphlets and Ephemera

Chamberlain's political career spanned almost fifty years, most of them spent in the eye of the storm. His passage from "fiery red" to "true blue" (to use the colours appended by Churchill) was turbulent with wrecked parties and abandoned causes trailing in his wake. Chamberlain was the most controversial British politician of his generation and was pursued to the end by the accusing cries of "Judas" and "turncoat". It will not surprise researchers that such a career generated an abundance of pamphlet literature and other ephemera, the largest collection of which is held at various locations in the Birmingham Collection at Birmingham Central Library. All facets of Chamberlain's politics are represented in the surviving pamphlet literature but there are heavy concentrations relating to education, Ireland and tariff reform.

A. EDUCATION, MUNICIPAL REFORM AND LIBERAL POLITICS TO 1886

It was the cause of free, compulsory, non-sectarian elementary education which drew Chamberlain into politics. He was intimately connected with the Birmingham Education League after 1867 and with its successor, the National Education League. A substantial collection of circulars, leaflets and other items published by the National Education League between 1869 and 1876 is held at Birmingham Central Library (accession number 68340). The League issued a numbered series of leaflets and no. 308, *The National Education League: Its Objects. Its Gains. Its Wants* (n.d.), provides a short summary of its policies. Researchers seeking an insight into the "caucus" system with which Chamberlain was so closely associated will find it clearly explained in a pamphlet written for the League by James Freeman on *The Cumulative Method of Voting* (1870), which includes an analysis of the voting pattern at the first Birmingham School Board election.

A number of Chamberlain's early speeches were published in pamphlet form by the National Education League. The most important is contained in *Verbatim Report of the Proceedings of a Deputation* which led Gladstone and Forster on 9 March 1870 to explain the League's objections to the Education Bill. Chamberlain was pre-occupied at this stage of his career with the perceived iniquity of rate support for Anglican schools and this is the main theme of, for example, *The Government and the Twenty-Fifth Clause of the Education Act* (1873). He also articulated nonconformist alarm regarding the religious education on offer as in the League's pamphlet *Religious Instruction in Board Schools* (1872).

Between 1873 and 1876 Chamberlain combined the chairmanship of the League's executive with the same role at the Birmingham School Board. The extent to which these roles overlapped is reflected in the League's pamphlets. Chamberlain's reflections on *Free Schools* (1875 and 1876) were published by the League as was a speech on the subject of rate-support for Church schools made at the School Board on 23 March 1876 which appeared under the title *Increase of Grants to Denominational Schools*. The League's *Monthly Paper*, which was issued between December 1869 and March 1877 provides a useful source for this phase of Chamberlain's career. Birmingham Central Library has a complete set at accession number 80291. Perhaps the most useful single pamphlet source on Chamberlain's career in educational politics is *Six Years of Educational Work in Birmingham*, published by the Birmingham School Board, which contains his valedictory address as retiring chairman delivered on 2 November 1876.

Chamberlain's regime as a radical, reforming mayor was marked by a number of pamphlets published by the Borough of Birmingham. The most important, perhaps, is *Proceedings on the Adoption by the Council of a Scheme for the Improvement of the Borough* (1875), which includes Chamberlain's key speech of 6 October. This may usefully be read alongside *The Progress of the Birmingham Improvement Scheme* (1878). Chamberlain's arguments in favour of municipal enterprise are neatly encapsulated in *Proceedings of the Town Council on the Reception of the Annual Report of the Gas Committee* (1879), in which he defends the profits generated and proposes to illuminate New Street. A critical perspective on the Birmingham improvement scheme is provided by a pamphlet written for the National Union of Conservative and Constitutional Associations by J.M. Brindley in 1885 on *The Homes of the Working Classes and the Promises of the Rt. Hon. J. Chamberlain, M.P.*

A minor Chamberlain theme from this period is evident in pamphlets which indicate his interest in public-house licensing reform along Scandinavian lines. *Licensing Reform and Local Option* (1876), published by the Birmingham Liberal Assocation, reprints a Chamberlain speech on this subject, and *Public House Reform* (1877) develops the arguments in response to a critical article on "The Birmingham Plan of Public House Reform" by Robert Lowe which had appeared in the January 1877 edition of the *Fortnightly Review*. Chamberlain's continuing interest is suggested by the pamphlet entitled *Public House Reform. Full Explanation of the Proposed Reform by the Rt. Hon. J. Chamberlain, M.P.* (1874), published by the Public House Reform Association, which reports a recent speech on the merits of the so-called "Gothenberg system".

Chamberlain carried his radicalism into parliament after 1876. As a politician with a national reputation it was not unusual for his speeches to appear in pamphlet form, often under the National Liberal Federation imprint. Particularly important here is his speech to the Federation's council on 22 January 1879, reprinted verbatim in the pamphlet containing the *First Annual Report*, which concludes with an attack on Hartington and the Whigs. As a member of Gladstone's Cabinet after 1880 his radicalism was somewhat constrained by the requirements of collective responsibility. He loyally toed the party line in *The Policy of the Government Since the General Election* (1881), a Federation pamphlet containing a speech delivered to his constituents on 7 June. *The Government and Its Assailants* (1883) is more provocative but his radical fire is directed principally at the Conservative opposition. Chamberlain's ministerial responsibilities at the Board of Trade are reflected in the Cobden Club pamphlet entitled *The French Treaty and Reciprocity* which repeats, with some revisions, his House of Commons speech in defence of free trade on 12 August 1881, a pronouncement which was to haunt him in later years. His battle with the shipowners over the Merchant Shipping Bill is evident in *Our Sailors*, the title given to Chamberlain's Commons speech of 19 May 1884, and the immediate response, *Merchant Shipping Legislation: A Reply* (1884), published by the Clyde Steamship Owners Association, which denied the charge that they sought to profit from over-insurance.

Hostile pamphleteers were not slow to identify the radical demon. *The Caucus Parliament. May 1880*, published anonymously, rehearsed the ultimate Tory nightmare—a Chamberlain Government with John Bright at the War Office and the spendthrift ex-Khedive of Egypt at the Treasury! A similar theme was developed later by A.R. Shipton in his pamphlet *The Fall of Brum. A Historical Pageant* (1886), which warned of dire consequences if the continuing rise of "Viscount Brum" remained unchecked. In addition, he was subjected to attacks by critics of various aspects of radical politics both before and after the appearance of "the unauthorised programme". Thus "A Tory Radical" in *A Letter to Joseph Chamberlain on the Unearned Increment* (1884) denounces Chamberlain as "a most unmitigated cad" for his attitude to aristocratic wealth.

Mr Chamberlain and the Taxation of the Working Classes (1885) reproduces an anonymous article from *The Economist* which challenges Chamberlain's assertion that the working class was more heavily taxed in proportion to income than the wealthy. Anglican critics were especially antagonistic in 1885–1886. The Rev. Thomas Morse published *Free Schools: A Reply to Some Recent Statements of the Rt. Hon. Joseph Chamberlain, M.P., and Others* (1885) criticising the commitment to free education in the unauthorised programme and George Denison, the Archdeacon of Taunton, in *Mr Chamberlain, June 1886*, characterised him as "the principal adversary of the Church of England". It should also be noted that Chamberlain came under fire from a fellow Liberal M.P., W.T. Marriot, in a pamphlet entitled *The Liberal Party and Mr Chamberlain* (1883 and 1884), which characterised him as a dangerous extremist. This might profitably be read in conjunction with the pseudonymous pamphlet by "Joseph", *Defeat and Retreat: Three Years Blunders* (1883), which attacks Gladstone's record from the perspective of a disenchanted radical.

B. IRELAND, THE LIBERAL SCHISM AND LIBERAL UNIONISM, 1886–1895

The Irish theme predominated in the years 1886–1890 as Chamberlain broke with Gladstone and then sought to establish a new political base. An important speech in Birmingham on 21 April 1886, just after his resignation, which outlines the reason for his departure, was published first by the Birmingham Liberal Association as *The Irish Policy of the Government* and then, later in the year, by the Liberal Unionist Committee as *Mr Chamberlain and the Birmingham Assocation*. The National Radical Union, to which Chamberlainites retreated after the breach with the National Liberal Federaton, also published a number of important speeches in pamphlet form. Of these, Chamberlain's *Speech* at Birmingham on 19 June 1886, in which he provides an account of his recent relations with Gladstone, and his speech at Hawick on 22 January 1887, published as *The Irish Question and the Reunion of the Liberal Party*, are especially worthy of attention. The Liberal Unionist Committee also published Chamberlain's 1886 Election Address under the title *The Government of Ireland Bill: Mr Chamberlain's Manifesto*. Numerous Chamberlain speeches and statements on Irish Home Rule are to be found in *The Case for the Union: A Collection of Leaflets, Pamphlets and Speeches on Home Rule for Ireland*, published by the Liberal Unionist Association in five series between 1887 and 1890, the most comprehensive coverage of the evolving Liberal Unionist position.

Amongst the more vigorous responses to Chamberlain's anti–Home Rule line were those of "Ignotus", an Irish Unionist advocate of land reform, in an open letter to Chamberlain published as *A United Kingdom Versus Home Rule Policy* (1886). More hostile was the pamphlet *Mr Chamberlain in Ulster* (1888), in which the Irish Nationalist, John Clancy, answered points raised by Chamberlain during his Ulster tour in the autumn of 1887. Chamberlain's former Liberal colleagues attacked on a broader front, denouncing him as the man who had wrecked his party. "Talus", the author of *Now or Never! A Letter to the Right Honourable ——* (1886), suggests, with leaden irony, that Chamberlain's destructive talents might be more appropriately maximised if he were to be elevated to the House of Lords. Isaac Latimer, editor of the Plymouth-based *Western Daily Mercury*, provides an excellent case study of Gladstonian fury in *Four Letters to the Rt. Hon. Joseph Chamberlain, M.P.* (1889), published after a speaking tour in the south-west. The most striking attack from this quarter, however, is the anonymous pamphlet entitled *The Coat of Many Colours* (1890), published by the Manchester-based National Reform Union and facetiously dedicated to the one-time advanced radical who was "now the devoted ally of Dukes and Duchesses".

As Liberal Unionism established itself as a significant parliamentary force and moved towards an alliance with the Conservatives the ephemera reflects Chamberlain's transitional position. The Cobden Club still claimed him as their own publishing a pamphlet on the *Sugar Bounty Convention* (1889) in which Chamberlain and Bright were cited as opponents of countervailing duties. The theme of social reform surfaced in a Birmingham speech advocating old age pensions and published in pamphlet form by the *Handsworth Chronicle* as *Friendly Societies and Old Age Pensions* (1894). *The Speech of Mr Chamberlain at Stourbridge*, delivered on 29 January 1894 and issued by the Midlands Liberal Unionist Association, marks the developing alliance with Salisbury with a stinging attack on the Liberal Government: "No House of Commons", he argues, "has ever done less". Files of *The Liberal Unionist* (1887–1892), published by the Liberal Unionist Association, provide a rich source for the Chamberlainite transition which led him from Gladstone's Government in 1886 to Salisbury's in 1895. The Bodleian Library has a set located at catalogue reference N 22957 c 5. Finally, in this section, William Sykes' pamphlet, *Before Joseph Came Into Egypt*, (1898), provides a useful, though hostile, summation of Chamberlain's career to this point with a compilation of selected extracts from speeches by or about Chamberlain designed to illustrate his fundamental inconsistency.

C. EMPIRE AND TARIFF REFORM, 1895–1914

Precursors of the debate which ensued after 1903 are evident from the time that Chamberlain took up his appointment as Colonial Secretary. His important speech at the Canada Club on 25 March 1896 exploring the possibility of imperial commercial union was published by the Imperial Federation (Defence) League under the title *The Rt. Hon. Joseph Chamberlain, M.P. . . . Imperial Federation*. Two Cobden Club leaflets, both published in 1896, indicate that the free trade alarm bells were ringing. *Australian Opinion on Mr Chamberlain's Scheme of British and Colonial Protection* cites press opposition to the *Zollverein* scheme. Lord Farrer's critique, *The Neo-Protectionist Scheme of the Rt. Hon. Joseph Chamberlain*, carried more weight. Thereafter, Chamberlain's involvement in South African affairs predominated as a pamphlet theme up to and beyond the outbreak of war in 1899. The extent of his complicity in the Jameson Raid was hotly debated. W.T. Stead of the *Review of Reviews* was sufficiently outraged to publish *The Scandal of the*

South African Committee (1899) and to bring out a second edition under the title *Joseph Chamberlain: Conspirator or Statesman?* (1900), with appendices containing fresh evidence against the Colonial Secretary. A reply based on Chamberlain's not entirely convincing denials was issued by the Women's Liberal Unionist Association with *Was Mr Chamberlain Privy to the Jameson Raid?* (1900).

Once the war was under way Liberal "pro-Boers" were determined to hold Chamberlain entirely responsible for the breakdown of negotiations with Kruger. This theme emerges clearly from C.A.V. Conybeare's pamphlet *Chamberlain's War* (1900), issued by the National Reform Union, and from H.A. Sykes Bickers' *Screw Diplomacy* (1901). Stead returned to the fray with a *Review of Reviews* penny pamphlet which promised *The Truth About the War* (1900) and argued that Chamberlain had been determined since 1895 to force the Boers into conflict. G.B. Clarke's pamphlet, entitled *The Offical Correspondence between the Governments of Great Britain, the South African Republic and the Orange Free State* (1900), is substantial and informative, especially on Chamberlain's crucial correspondence with Milner. Chamberlain's most notable contribution to the debate on the conduct of the war was to reply to the "methods of barbarism" charge raised by Campbell-Bannerman and others. This was published as *Mr Chamberlain's Defence of British Troops in South Africa against the Foreign Slanders* (1902).

The pamphlet literature and other ephemera generated by Chamberlain's final crusade for tariff reform and imperial preference is vast. Its volume bears testimony, in part, to the difficulties experienced by the tariff reformers as they struggled to detach the electorate from habits of thought embedded in the conventional wisdom of successive generations since the time of Cobden and Bright. It also reflects the size of the task confronted by Chamberlain's opponents as they re-educated themselves and the public in the defence of economic doctrines which had long been taken for granted.

For a researcher unfamiliar with this territory the most useful starting point is provided by the various organisations which were ranged behind tariff reform and free trade after 1903. The London-based Tariff Reform League issued two kinds of campaign literature. Much of its output was aimed at the dedicated activist and designed to provide the Chamberlainite canvasser or street-corner orator with arguments and statistics. The League, which is heavily listed in the catalogues of the British Library, the British Library of Political and Economic Science and the Bodleian Library, published *Monthly Notes on Tariff Reform* each month from July 1904 to July 1914 with the activist in mind. It also prepared at least seven editions between 1903 and 1911 of a substantial *Short Handbook for Speakers and Students of the Policy of Preferential Tariffs*. In addition, it flooded the country with leaflets. Useful samples, described as "Specimen Leaflets", from 1908 and 1909 are held at the Bodleian Library at reference 23226 d 41 (19,20). These include typical approaches to special industrial interests, such as *Facts About the Boot and Shoe Trade* and *What Preference Means to British Tweed Workers*, as well as *A Word to Tea Drinkers* and other leaflets aimed at a wider audience. It should be noted that the work of the Tariff Reform League was paralleled until July 1911 by the Birmingham-based Imperial Tariff Committee which issued its own version of *Monthly Notes* and at least one edition, in 1905, of the *Short Handbook*, the fiscal reformers' Bible.

They were answered by a battery of pro–free trade groups closely asssociated with the Liberal Party, notably the Cobden Club, the Free Tade Union and the Liberal Legue. Though the work of the Free Trade Union, directed by Harold Cox, was closest in style and range to that of the Tariff Reform League, the most considered responses appeared under the Cobden Club imprint. An interesting group of Cobden Club leaflets dating from mid 1903 and held by the Bodleian Library (at reference 23226 e 52) provide useful explorations of the imperial aspects of Chamberlain's policy; *The Burden of Empire*, for example, links the genesis of tariff reform to Chamberlain's failure to secure colonial co-operation in imperial defence. The most important Cobden Club publications, however, confronting Chamberlain's policy in sustained argument, are *Fact versus Fiction: The Cobden Club's Reply to Mr Chamberlain* (1904) and a short book advertised as its sequel, *Tariff Makers: Their Aims and Methods* (1909). Both appear to be largely the work of H. Shaw-Lefevre (Lord Everlsey). Chamberlain's version of industrial decline was explicitly challenged in another Cobden Club publication, J.M. Robertson's *The Collapse of Tariff Reform: Mr Chamberlain's Case Exposed* (1911). Socialist responses to the new policy are indicated in Philip Snowden's Independent Labour Party pamphlet *The Chamberlain Bubble* (1903) and also Joe Walker's *Socialism versus the Chamberlain Red Herring* (1904).

Chamberlain's speeches were often issued in pamphlet form by sympathetic campaign organisations. His great Birmingham speech of 15 May 1903, for example, was published by the Birmingham Liberal Unionist Association with the title *Imperial Federation*. It contains not only a verbatim account of the speech but a useful synopsis of key points. The Glasgow speech of 6 October 1903 in which Chamberlain outlined the details of his policy for the first time was published as *The Policy of Imperial Preference* by the Imperial Tariff Committee. The Liberal free trade platform response is most usefully addressed by following the speeches of Asquith who dogged Chamberlain throughout his various speaking tours. Four Asquith speeches from October 1903, indicative of thousands of others on the free trade side and containing cross-references to Chamberlain's declarations, were published as *Trade and the Empire: Mr Chamberlain's Proposals Examined* (1903).

Fiscal policy pamphleteers flourished in the years after 1903 as tariff reform temporarily eclipsed other political issues. Amongst the most able defenders of the *status quo* was the economist A.C. Pigou who supplied a notably cool and critical review of Chamberlain's proposals in *The Great Inquest, An Examination of Mr Chamberlain's Fiscal Proposals* and *The Riddle of the Tariff*, both published in 1903. Bartholomew Smith's *Chamberlain and Chamberlainism: His Fiscal Proposals and Colonial Policy* was fiercely hostile but notable for setting tariff reform in the context of Chamberlain's performance as Colonial Secretary. Harold Storey's *The*

Argument for Free Trade Re-examined and Re-stated in the Light of Mr Chamberlain's Attack (1904) is especially scathing on Chamberlain's imperial preference proposals. Other free trade pamphleteers focused on tariff reform as the thin end of the protectionist wedge, a line pursued by the *Daily News* journalist G.H. Perris in *The Protectionist Peril: An Examination of Mr Chamberlain's Proposals* (1903) and by J. Rigby Smith in his well-argued *Mr Chamberlain's Defence of Colonial Protection* (1904), which claims that Chamberlain's speeches "disclosed a technical ignorance of economics". J.M. Robertson's *Chamberlain: A Study* (1905) is notable largely for the sustained hostility generated throughout its sixty-four pages, which concludes with the helpful advice that Chamberlain should retire. As the 1906 election approached free traders redoubled their efforts to embarrass their arch foe with evidence of his fiscal apostasy. A compilation of apparently contradictory quotations, assembled by Alexander Mackintosh for this purpose, was published in December 1905 under the title *Joseph Chamberlain on Both Sides: A Book of Contrasts*.

Amongst Chamberlain's most articulate defenders were Walter Hammond whose *Thoughts on Mr Chamberlain's Proposed Fiscal Policy* (1903) noted American and German progress behind tariff walls. "Regulator" dedicated *The Present Position of the Empire* (1903) to Chamberlain as the "only man" capable of securing the goal of imperial consolidation. For a classic restatement of the Chamberlainite case in the words of one of his foremost disciples reseachers might turn to Leo Amery's *The Case for Tariff Reform* (1905). Some pamphlets aimed to inform rather than to proselytise. Useful examples in this category include *The Fiscal Puzzle: Both Sides Explained by Leading Men*, (1903), which has the attraction of cartoon illustrations by Carruthers-Gould of the *Westminster Gazette*, and T.L. Gilmour's *All Sides of the Fiscal Policy* (1903), an indexed collection of extracts from twenty-one key speeches delivered betwen May and November 1903.

Finally, it should be noted that the tariff reform–free trade controversy spawned a curious sub-genre in the form of humorous (or supposedly humorous) pamphlets. Amongst these whimsical contributions to Edwardiana on the pro–tariff reform side is J.S. Fletcher's *Owd Poskitt: His Opinions on Mr Chamberlain and on English Trade in General* (1903), which records the response of a fictional English farmer to the tariff scheme. This is balanced by David O'Drumcavil's *Farthing Joe* (1904), which envisages Chamberlain in conversation with "Sandie Broon" and caught out by his homespun free trade arguments. *Talking it Over* by J. Middleton (1905) uses the common sense of the Lancashire artisan to punch holes in the tariff proposals. This vein is further explored by "A Man Fra' Sheffield" in *Playing Mr Chamberlain's Game* (1903). Mercifully its wit is less ponderous and less pretentious than in Mark Gordon's *"Joe", or a Crisis in Dr Munden's School* (1903), a self-styled "fiscallegory" in which John Bull learns the benefits of self defence, or in "Anglo Saxon's" Biblical parody *Joseph the Deliverer of the Land of Egypt* (1903). The cause of poetry is not advanced by "A Free Trade Rhymer" with sixty-four laboured stanzas attacking *The Fiscal Piper of Brum* (1904). Neither is the art of the comic novel well-served by Paul Herring's fiscal farce *The Wrong Mr Chamberlain* (1904).

Chapter Eleven

Contemporary Newspapers

Chamberlain's position at the centre of controversy in the late nineteenth and early twentieth centuries ensured that he was amongst the most widely reported politicians of his time. Millions of printed words and thousands of column inches were devoted to Chamberlain's speeches, often reproduced verbatim, and to news and comment relating to his policies and manoeuvres. It is also important to recognise that Chamberlain's commitment to democratic politics led him into an active relationship with the press. He was not merely a passive recipient of press coverage but sought to influence its contents. "Chamberlain", as Collard has noted, "assiduously cultivated journalistic contacts and was quite willing to draft articles for publication".[1] As a Cabinet minister he leaked profusely, mainly for the benefit of the *Birmingham Daily Post*.

The first problem confronting any researcher contemplating this voluminous and complex source is where to begin. In most instances particular requirements will determine the starting point. For example, researchers seeking to follow aspects of Chamberlain's career through the local press will find it useful to consult Gibson, J., *Local Newspapers 1750–1920—England and Wales: A Select Location Guide*, (Birmingham, 1987). An interest in Chamberlain's foray at the 1874 general election would lead naturally to the *Sheffield Daily Telegraph*, the Conservative newspaper credited with temporarily thwarting his parliamentary ambitions. Similarly, a researcher anxious to locate Chamberlain in the hagiography of Birmingham radicalism could do worse than to consult the *Pall Mall Gazette*'s "Extra" of 18 November 1883, issued on the occasion of the "John Bright Celebration" and providing extensive coverage of Chamberlain's speech and his part in the proceedings.

More generally, researchers would be well-advised to start with *The Times*, not least because of the availability of Palmer's detailed *Index*, an invaluable aid. *Times* coverage of the major political events and issues of the period was both authoritative and comprehensive with an editorial line which became increasingly sympathetic towards Chamberlain as he made the transition from "Radical Joe" to imperial statesman. Leads from this indexed source may then, of course, be tracked through other contemporary newspapers as appropriate.

Of these, the most significant is the *Birmingham Daily Post* with which Chamberlain had a special relationship, well-documented in Whates' informative centenary volume.[2] The *Post*'s editor between 1862 and 1899 was J.T. Bunce, a trusted mentor of the National Education League and its leaders, also "the intimate personal friend of the most important of them".[3] Leading articles for the *Post* were often written by William Harris, sometimes referred to as the originator of the Birmingham Liberal "Caucus"; later Charles Vince, Chamberlain's Liberal Unionist agent, was a frequent contributor. Chamberlain himself provided copy for the *Post*, supplying, for example, a series on "The Condition of Ireland" in 1888. Alfred Robbins, London correspondent of the *Post* after 1885, enjoyed "close and friendly" relations with Chamberlain. It is not surprising, therefore, that the *Post* shifted from Liberalism to Liberal Unionism in June 1887 thus helping to secure the foundations of Chamberlain's West Midlands "Duchy". The *Post*, however, was not slavish in its devotion. On tariff reform it pursued a cautious Balfourite policy after May 1903, only capitulating to Chamberlain after a change of editor in November 1905. In Birmingham Chamberlain could normally rely on a sympathetic press, especially after the Liberal *Daily Argus* had been absorbed by the *Birmingham Daily Gazette* in 1903. At the 1906 election Birmingham Liberals were forced to publish their own campaign newspaper, the *Birmingham Election News*, in a vain attempt to counter the tariff reform influence. "At present", it was noted in its edition of 4 January, "all the Birmingham newspapers are singing the same song, and that song is—Mr Chamberlain".

In evaluating individual newspapers as sources for Chamberlain's career the researcher has to cultivate a sensitivity to changing affiliations. Liberal newspapers, such as the *Daily News*, the *Manchester Guardian* and the *Pall Mall Gazette*, which provided Chamberlain with generally sympathetic treatment before 1886, did not follow the *Birmingham Daily Post* into Liberal Unionism and opposed him vehemently thereafter. During the Boer War Chamberlain was especially irritated by the stance of the Cadbury-owned *Daily News* which, abandoned liberal imperialism for an anti-war stance.[4] The Conservative dailies experienced this transformation in reverse. The *Morning Post*, for example, which had once thundered against the politics of "ransom" was "more 'Joeite' than Joe himself" by 1906.[5] It should also be noted that the London *Standard* switched its editorial line from free trade to tariff reform when it was bought for the Chamberlainite cause by C. Arthur Pearson in November 1904. Pearson, chairman of the Tariff Reform League, thereby silenced the only Unionist free trade voice amongst the London dailies. He also started a number of newspapers in the tariff reform interest, notably the *Birmingham Gazette and Express* and the Newcastle *Evening Mail*. His flagship, the *Daily Express*, provided the most consistent support for Chamberlain's new policy after May 1903.

There are, in addition to the files of national and provincial newspapers for the period held at the British Library Newspaper Library and elsewhere, some useful collections of newspaper cuttings relevant to Chamberlain's career. The most significant are to be found amongst the Chamberlain papers at Birmingham University Library, mainly in boxes JC4/1–13, which relate to speeches and other political activities arranged by subject for the period 1868–1914. There are further boxes of cuttings at JC1/17/1 relating to Chamberlain's ancestry and early years, at JC3/5/1–50 relating to the Washington Fisheries Conference of 1887–1888, at JC6/7/1–173 on general political matters from 1880–1905, at JC8/10/1–42 on Irish home rule in 1886–1887 and 1893–1894, at JC9/6/3F/1–5 on West Africa in 1895–1899, at JC 12/3/1–62 relating to political and other honours in 1898–1902 and at JC18/18/1–155 on fiscal policy in 1903. Some additional cuttings, including obituaries from 1914 and later material linked to Chamberlain's centenary in 1936, are located at JC23/1/1–7 and JC24/1/1–2.

The Local Studies Department at Birmingham Central Library also holds some relevant collections of newspaper cuttings, usually in scrapbook form. The most important (with accession numbers in parentheses) are: cuttings relating to the National Education League, 1869 (68385); cuttings relating to Joseph Chamberlain, 1874 (304788); portraits and cartoons of Joseph Chamberlain, c. 1880–1906 (302131); cuttings relating to Chamberlain's farewell and return to Birmingham after his South African tour, 1902–1903 (174049) and cuttings relating to his visit to Glasgow, 1903 (453973). There is also a volume of cartoons, mainly of Chamberlain, dating from c. 1895–1906, collected by J. Macmillan (302126), and also five useful scrapbooks, arranged by theme, collected by G.H. Osborne. One of these relates specifically to Chamberlain and contains material dating from the period 1863–1909 (243132). The others are concerned with the Birmingham parliamentary election of 1880, (286536), the Gas department, water and parks (243371). Finally, there is some useful material on the parliamentary election of 1880 to be found in volumes 21 and 22 of the collection made by Sir John Benjamin Stone (279526).

NOTES

1. C.L. Collard, "Tariff Reform, Politics and the Press—Birmingham 1903–1906", *West Midland Studies* 16 (1983), 16.

2. H.R.G. Whates, *The Birmingham Post 1857–1957* (Birmingham, 1957), 114–126, 168–182. A collection of leading articles from the *Birmingham Daily Post* from 1867 to 1898 has been deposited in the Local Studies Department of Birmingham Central Library, accession number 273258.

3. Whates, 80–81.

4. See S. Koss, *The Rise and Fall of the Political Press in Britain* Volume I (Hamish Hamilton, 1981), 397–400.

5. See Koss Volume II (Hamish Hamilton, 1984), 67.

Author Index

Entries refer to item numbers, not page numbers.

Subject Index

Entries refer to item numbers, not page numbers.

About the Compilers

SCOTT NEWTON is Dean of the Faculty of Humanities and Social Sciences at the University of Wales, College of Cardiff. He is the coauthor, with Dilwyn Porter, of *Modernization Frustrated: The Politics of Economic Decline in Britain since 1900* (1988).

DILWYN PORTER is Senior Lecturer in History at Worcester College. He is the coauthor, with Scott Newton, of *Modernization Frustrated: The Politics of Economic Decline in Britain since 1900* (1988).

Recent Titles in
Bibliographies and Indexes in World History

France under the German Occupation, 1940–1944: An Annotated Bibliography
Donna Evleth, compiler

A World in Turmoil: An Integrated Chronology of the Holocaust and World War II
Hershel Edelheit and Abraham J. Edelheit

First-Person Accounts of Genocidal Acts Committed in the Twentieth Century: An Annotated Bibliography
Samuel Totten

A Catalogue of Audio and Video Collections of Holocaust Testimony—Second Edition
Joan Ringelheim, compiler

A Guide to East Asian Collections in North America
Thomas H. Lee, compiler

World Racism and Related Inhumanities: A Country-by-Country Bibliography
Meyer Weinberg, compiler

A Selected Bibliography of Modern Historiography
Attila Pók, editor

The Rise and Fall of the Soviet Union: A Selected Bibliography of Sources in English
Abraham J. Edelheit and Hershel Edelheit, editors

History of Canadian Childhood and Youth: A Bibliography
Neil Sutherland, Jean Barman, and Linda L. Hale, compilers

Contemporary Canadian Childhood and Youth: A Bibliography
Neil Sutherland, Jean Barman, and Linda L. Hale, compilers

Spanish and Portuguese Jewry: A Classified Bibliography
Robert Singerman, compiler

Crime in Victorian Britain: An Annotated Bibliography from Nineteenth-Century British Magazines
E. M. Palmegiano, compiler

www.ingramcontent.com/pod-product-compliance
Lightning Source LLC
Chambersburg PA
CBHW020355100426
42812CB00001B/68
* 9 7 8 0 3 1 3 2 8 2 9 0 4 *